Paint by Numbers
Coloring Pixel & Areas Book
Volume 1

Smart Things Begin With Griddlers.net
Copyright © All Rights Reserved. www.griddlers.net

Paint by Numbers - Coloring Pixel & Areas Book (Volume 1)

Published by: Griddlers.net
a division of A.A.H.R. Offset Maor Ltd

Copyright © Griddlers.net. All rights reserved. Printed in the US. No part of this book may be used or reproduced in any manner whatsoever without written permission except in the case of brief quotations embodied in critical articles or reviews.

Author: Griddlers Team
Compiler: Rastislav Rehák
Cover design: Elad Maor
Cover background elements by: freepic
Contributors: abrek, aga0211p, Amoebe, animgirl, any_anthony, arcadedweller, bart88, Belf_, beren2005, bombastico, carm53, Christophine, Comicpainter, desmo, DrDoris, Eilleen, elimaor, f1comp, Glucklich, goodgirl, griddlock, hi19hi19, hibrahimozer, jana11, Jasomslovak, Joopie, kendrasong, kikiki, LateXD, ld5, ledka, Lenchik, lilyania, Maedhros, MagdalenaAlb, maristone, memnune, Minoo, Misty, mudshark, nasa17, Nicky, NiunQa, notorioushat, op1, oren, paffy, popkin, powerpuffgrl65, r_shai, Rainbow15, rapa100, ravenmb, sablett, schmook1773, skybreezes, starch, stdesign, stetsonic, stumpy, talanimal, TNT, ulka, vivimagi, vtipkarjope, wiggles, willem, wylwo2, xxLadyJxx, yeu, zjmonty

ISBN: 978-9657679265

More information:
Email – team@griddlers.net
Website – http://www.griddlers.net

About Paint by Numbers

These coloring pictures are made of original griddlers puzzles. Though the puzzles themselves requires logic to solve them, the results are always very nice images. For those of you who prefer to relax when solving puzzles we decided to convert these nice images into a coloring book.

There are color names under each puzzle which can sometimes seem strange, however you can find colors by names on the back cover of this book. This palette comes from a popular set of colors. You can use any similar color.

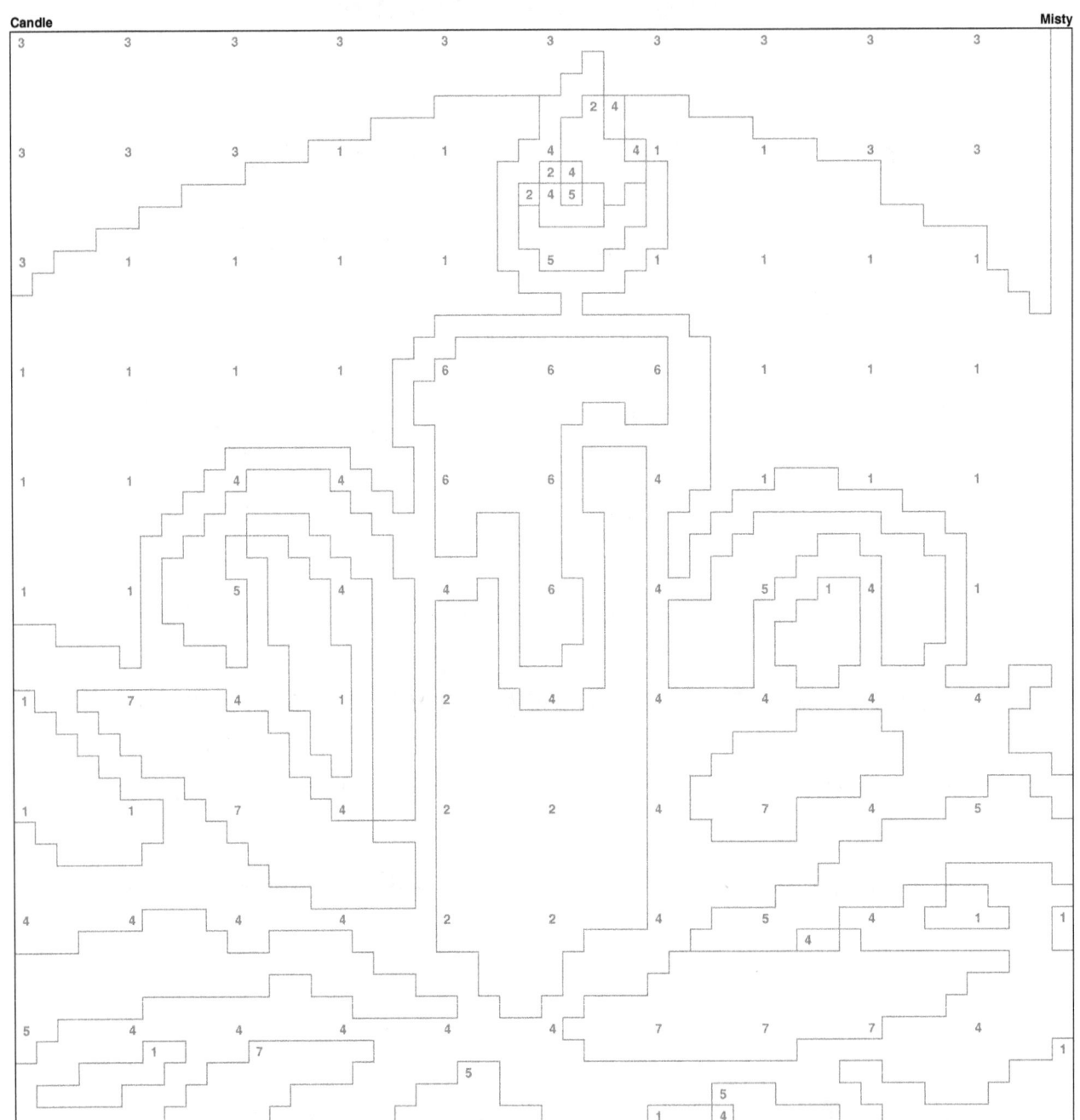

1-Cornflower, 2-Yellow, 3-Midnight Blue, 4-Black, 5-Scarlet, 6-White, 7-Mountain Meadow

Arkansas Razorbacks TNT

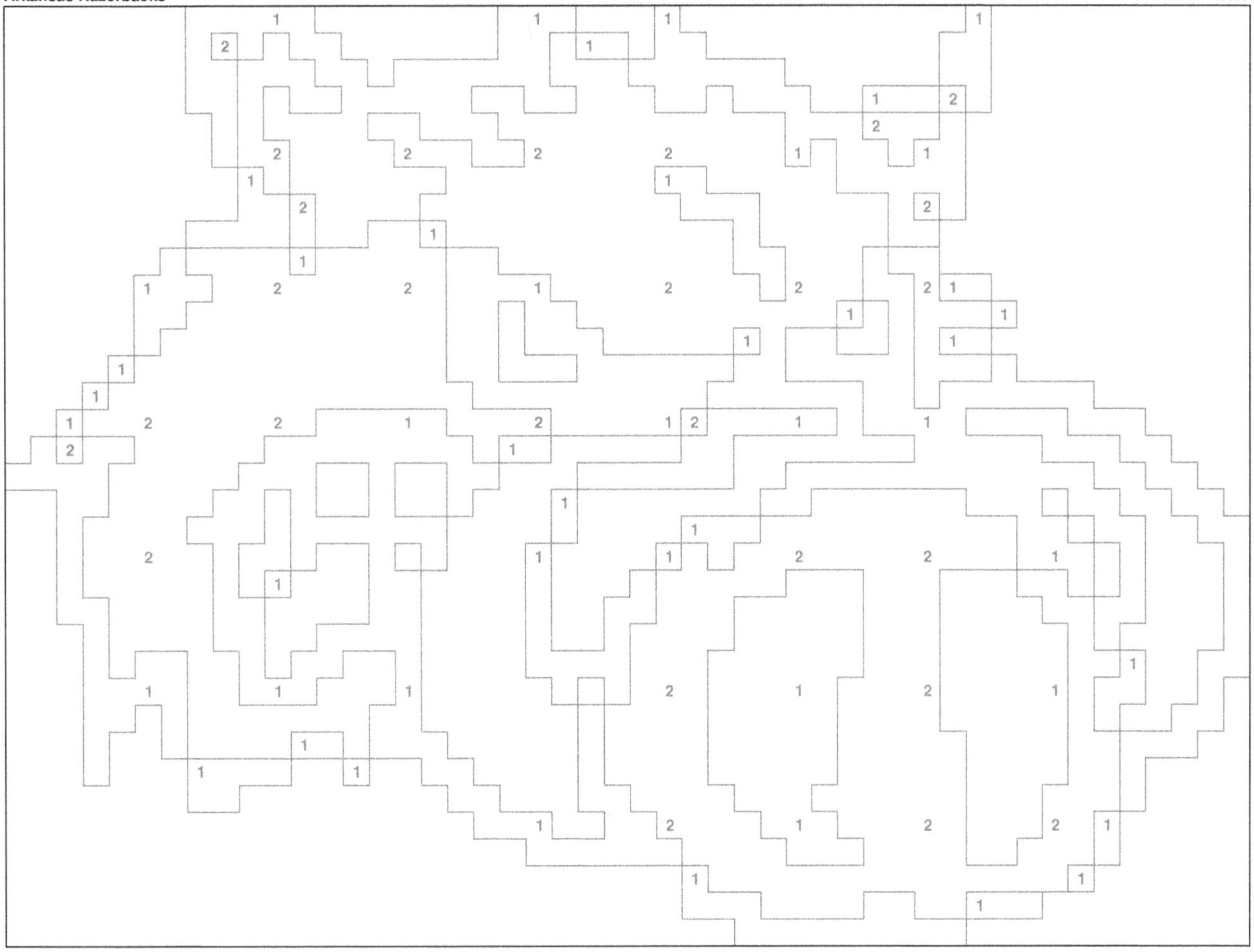

1-Black, 2-Fuzzy Wuzzy

Laundry hibrahimozer

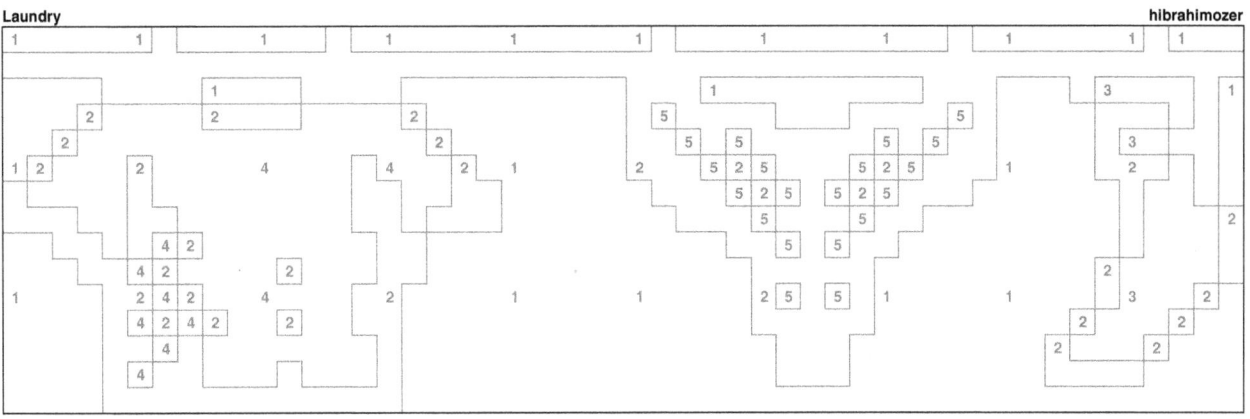

1-Periwinkle, 2-Black, 3-Green, 4-Scarlet, 5-Manatee

...and The City   goodgirl

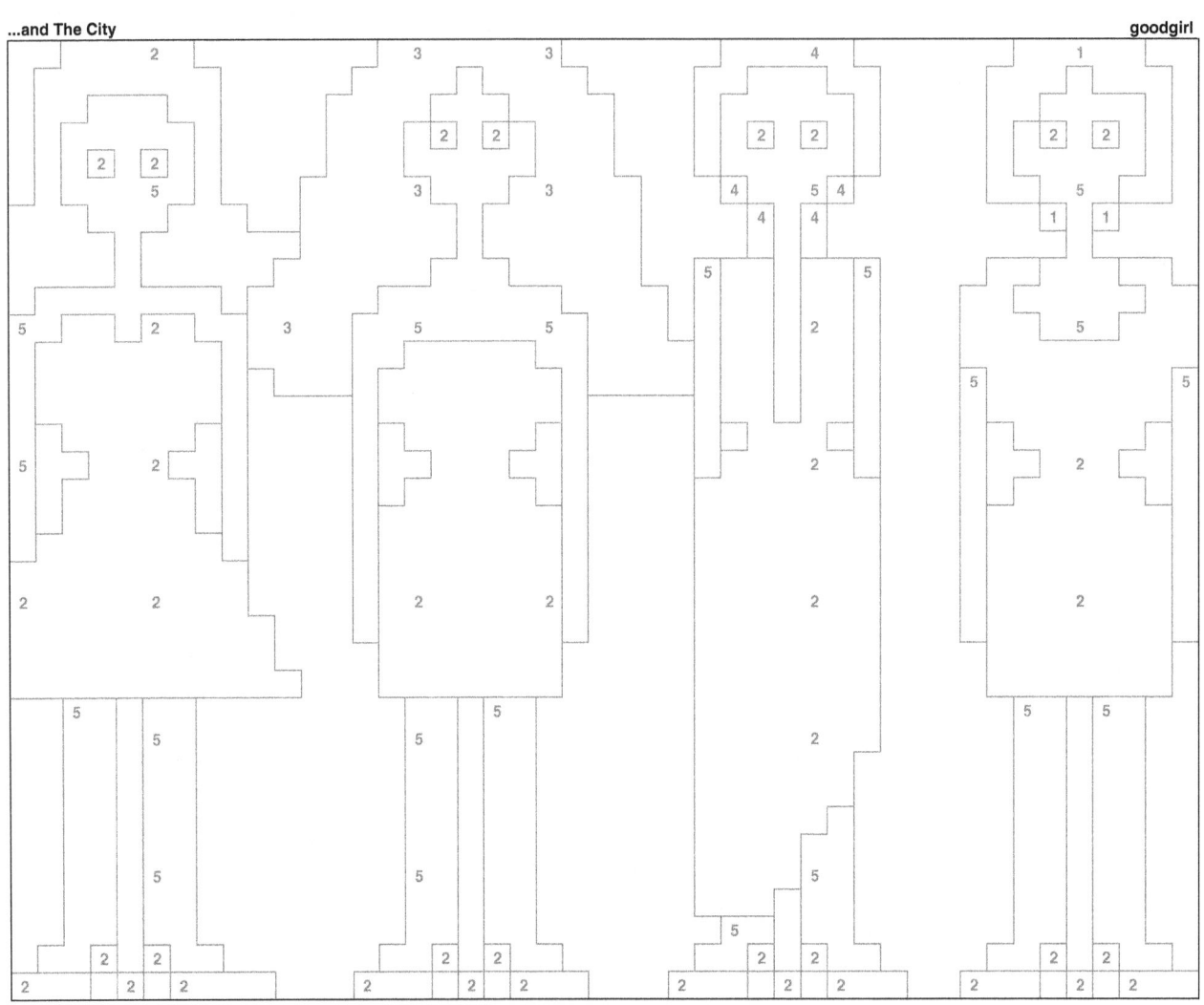

1-Mango Tango, 2-Black, 3-Raw Sienna, 4-Yellow-Orange, 5-Pig Pink

You Are Good! r_shai

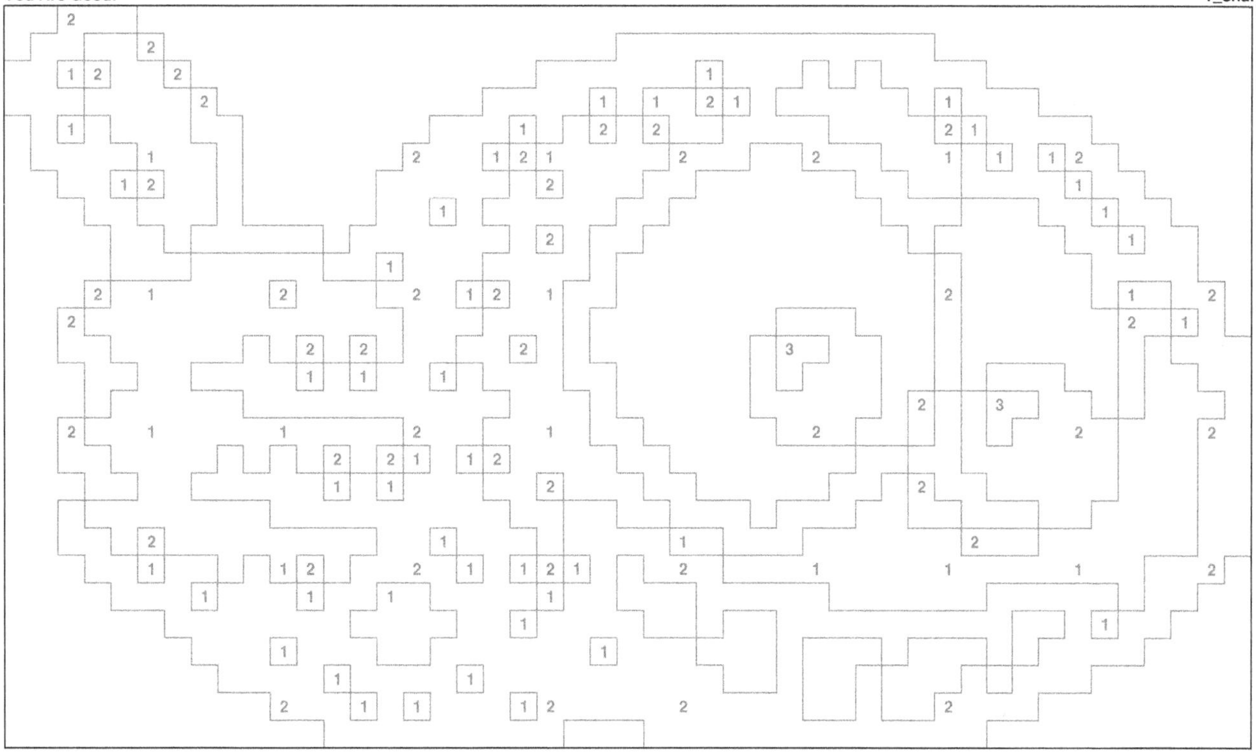

1-Dandelion, 2-Black, 3-Robin's Egg Blue

Ford Focus f1comp

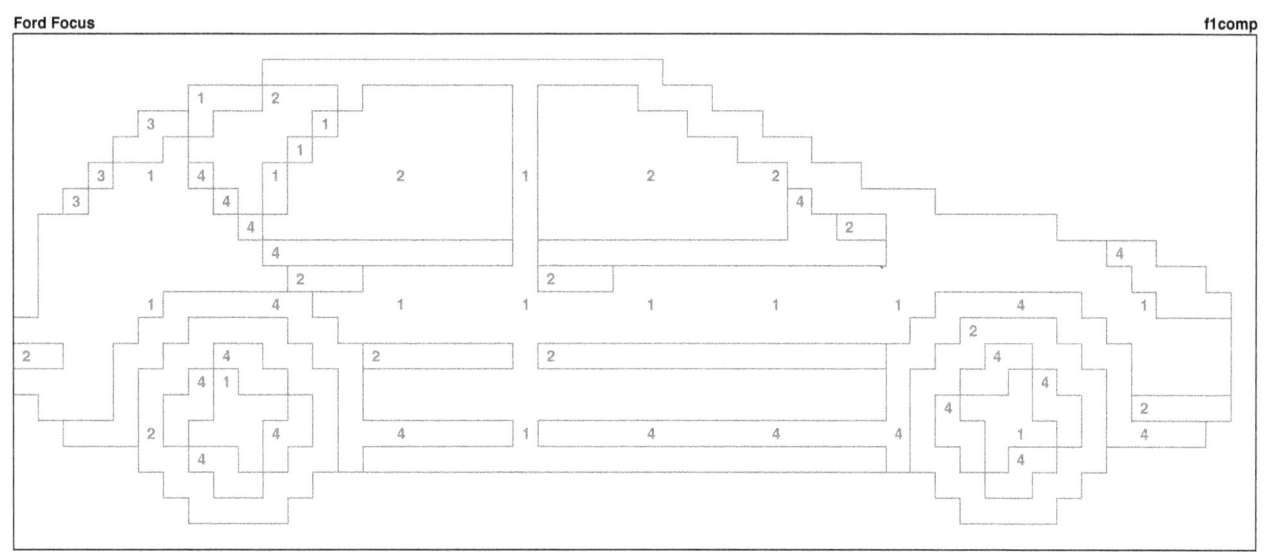

1-Manatee, 2-Black, 3-Scarlet, 4-Periwinkle

Oldie But Goodie powerpuffgrl65

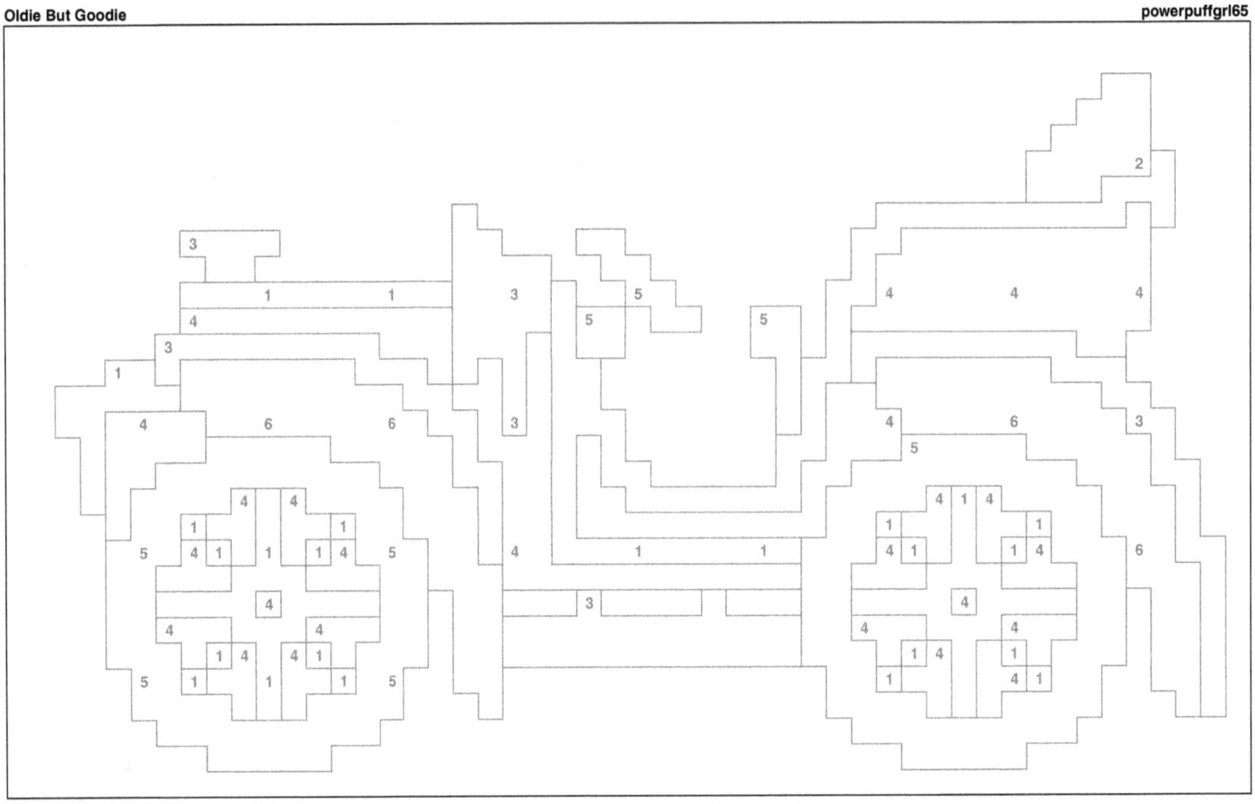

1-Scarlet, 2-Lavender (II), 3-Dandelion, 4-Navy Blue, 5-Black, 6-Midnight Blue

Pink Panther sablett

1-Periwinkle, 2-Black, 3-Canary, 4-Maroon, 5-Tickle Me Pink, 6-Pig Pink

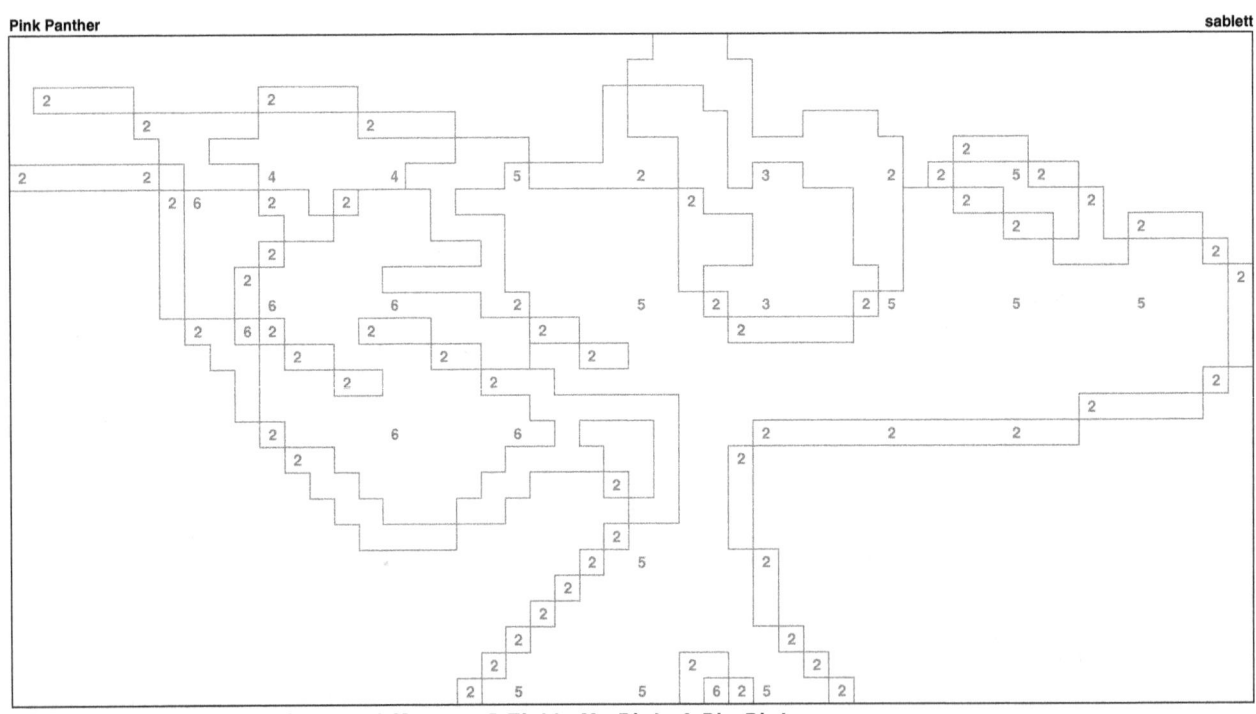

Doggy — Jasomslovak

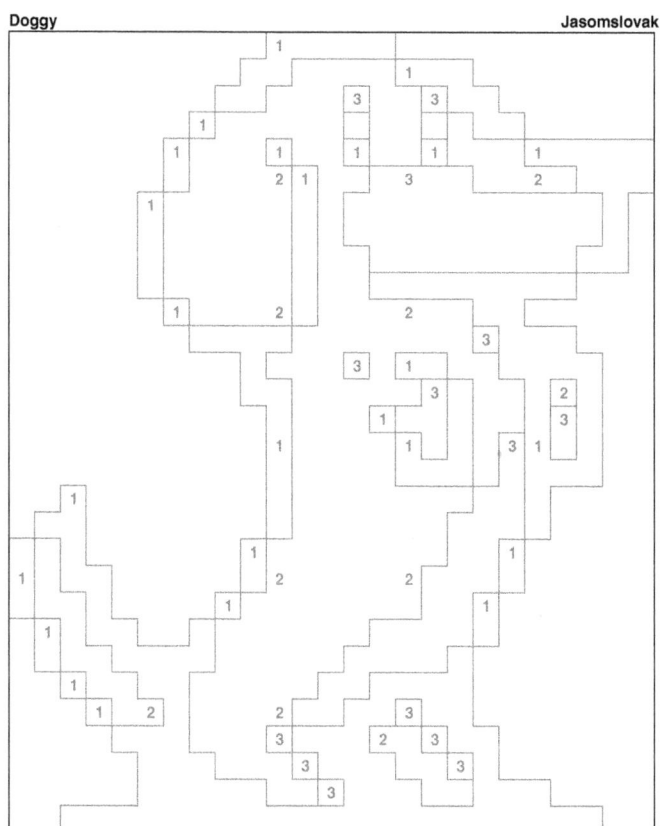

1-Black, 2-Fuzzy Wuzzy, 3-Mango Tango

Purple — Nicky

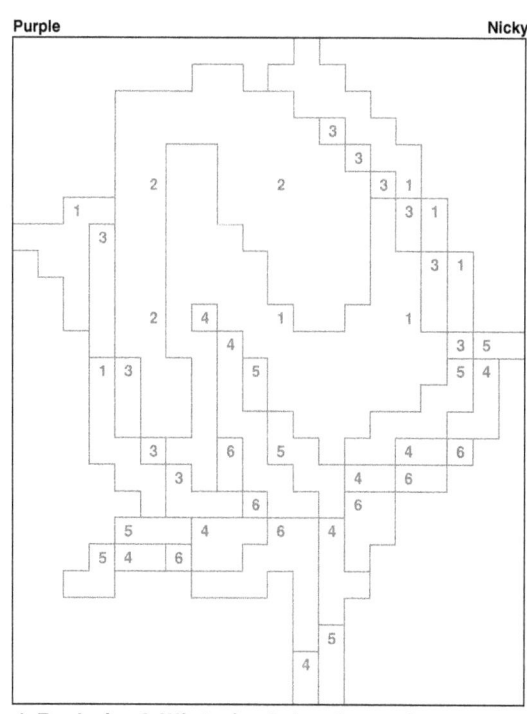

1-Fuchsia, 2-Wisteria, 3-Jazzberry Jam, 4-Green, 5-Caribbean Green, 6-Tropical Rain Forest

Cherry Blossom — Nicky

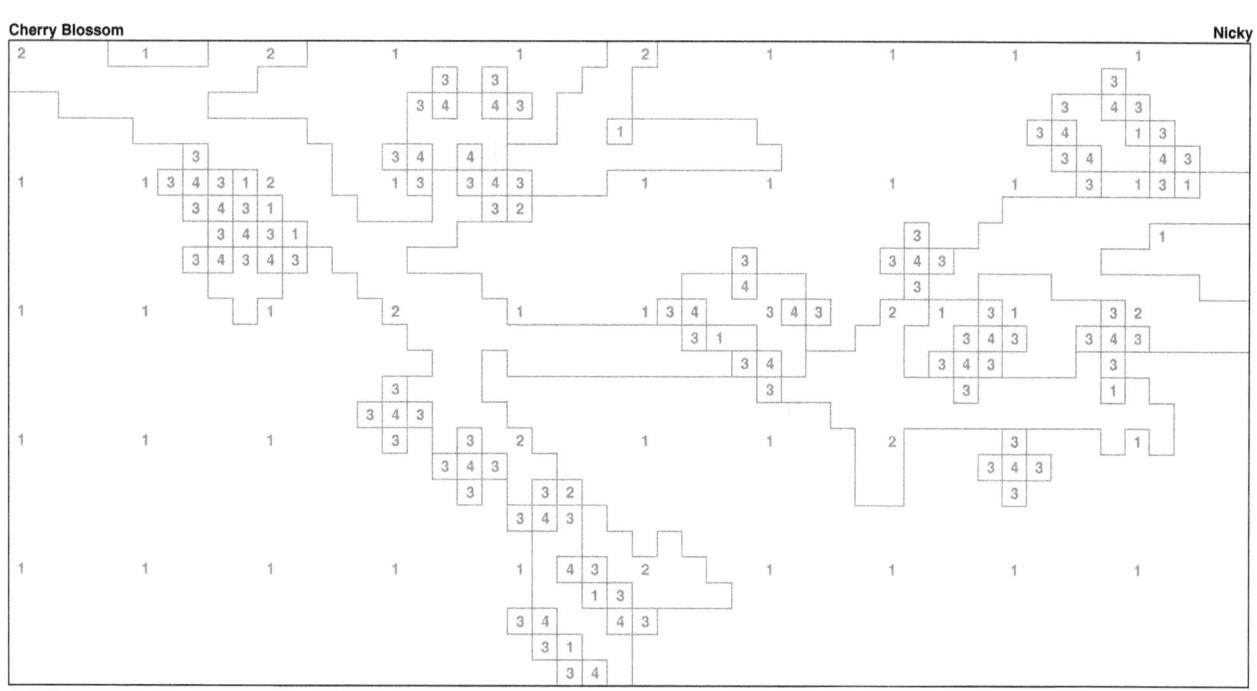

1-White, 2-Eggplant, 3-Tickle Me Pink, 4-Lavender (II)

Nevada-Las Vegas Rebels — TNT

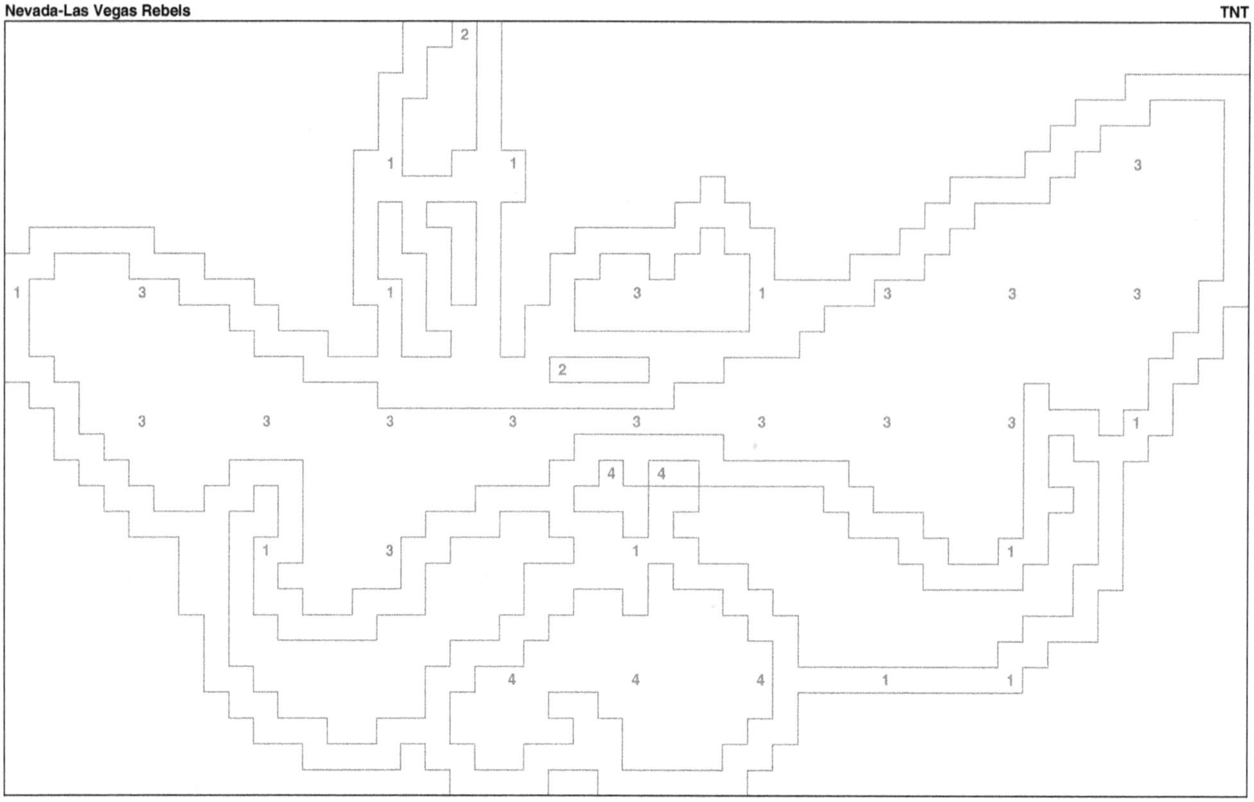

1-Black, 2-Scarlet, 3-Timberwolf, 4-Peach

Pipe — Belf

1-Black, 2-Eggplant, 3-Shadow, 4-Brown, 5-Dandelion

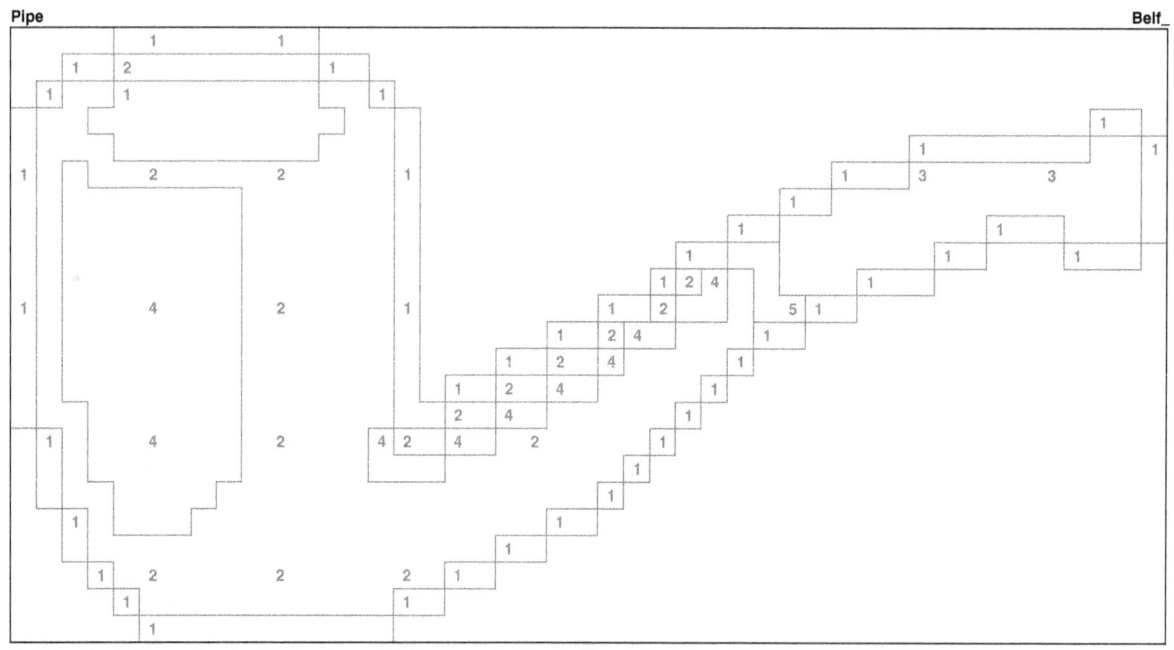

www.griddlers.net — Paint by Numbers, Vol. 1

Owl — Nicky

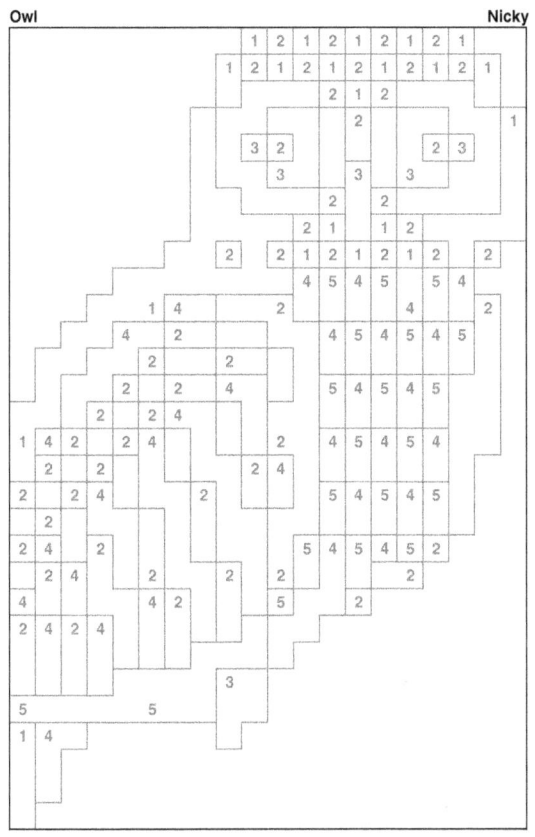

1-Mahogany, 2-Eggplant, 3-Dandelion,
4-Brown, 5-Mango Tango

Lisa Simpson — yeu

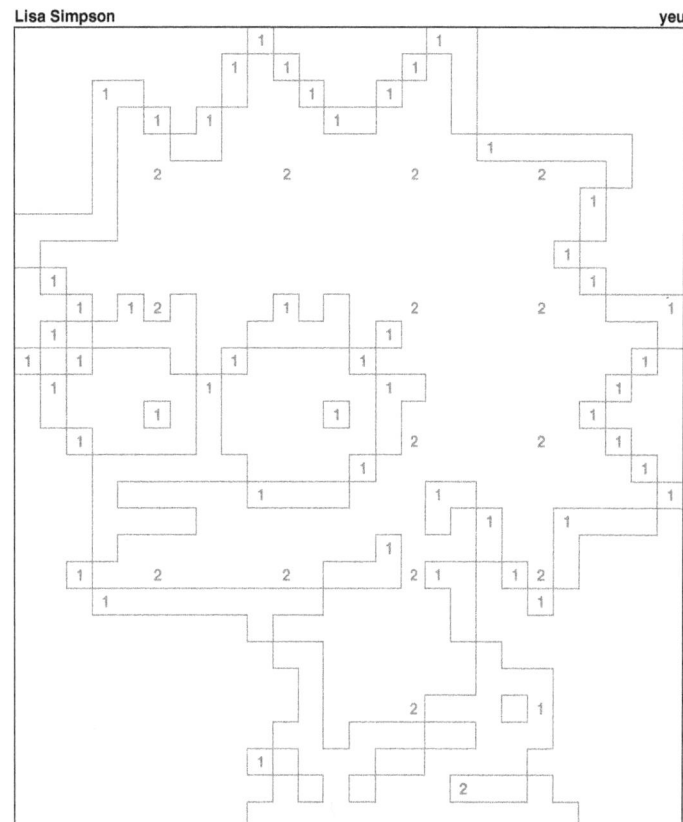

1-Black, 2-Dandelion

Four Chicks — kendrasong

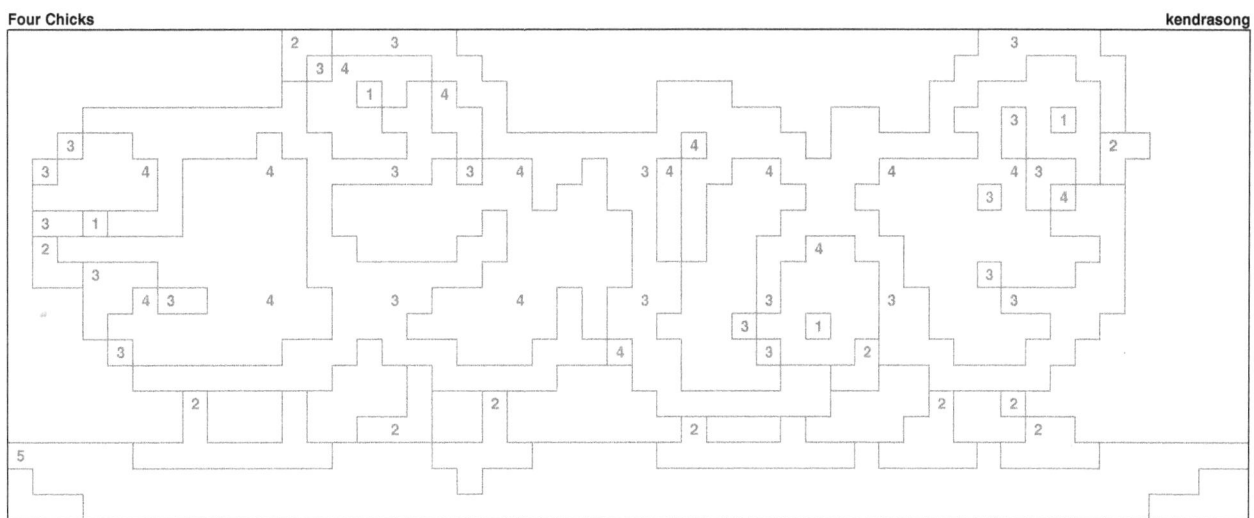

1-Black, 2-Red-Orange, 3-Yellow-Orange, 4-Dandelion, 5-Green

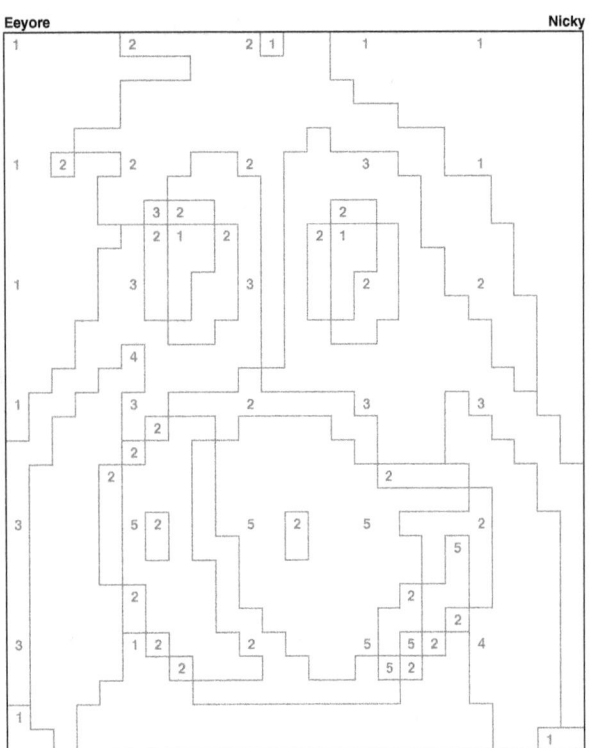

1-White, 2-Outer Space, 3-Blue Bell, 4-Wild Strawberry, 5-Peach

1-Jazzberry Jam, 2-Outer Space, 3-Beaver, 4-Banana Mania, 5-Mango Tango

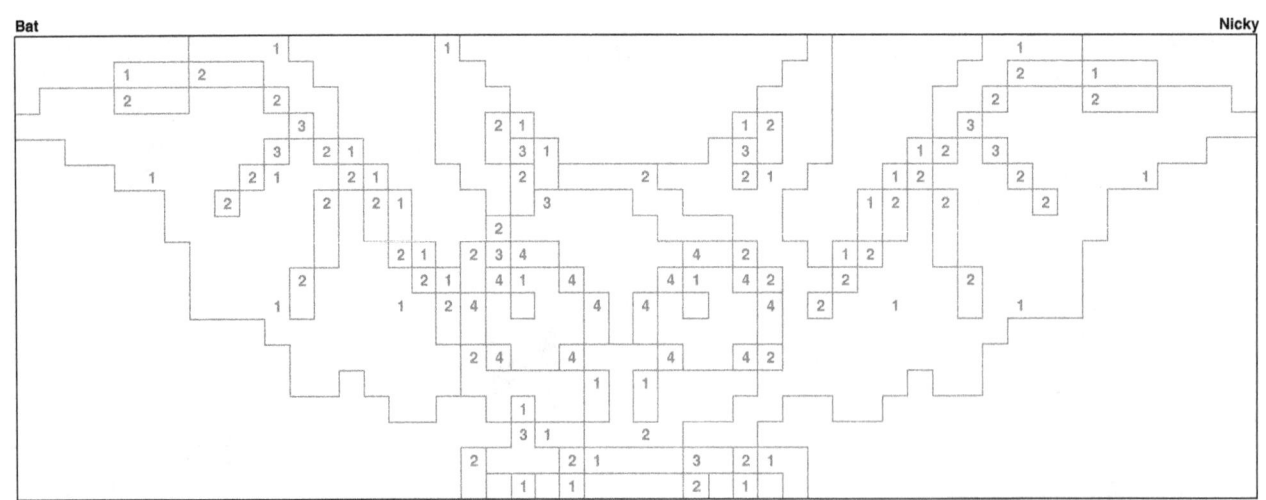

1-Black, 2-Shadow, 3-Manatee, 4-Timberwolf

Bear With Bow — Nicky

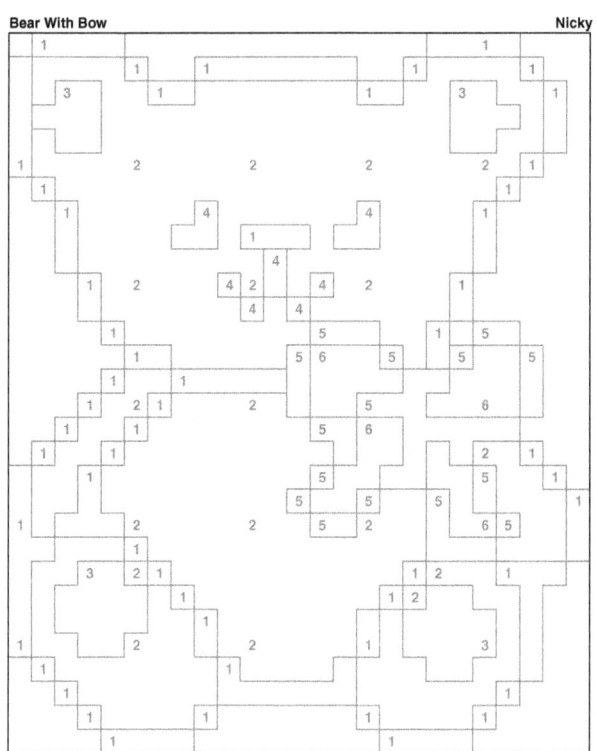

1-Brown, 2-Olive Green, 3-Desert Sand, 4-Shadow,
5-Bittersweet, 6-Melon

Red Rose — Nicky

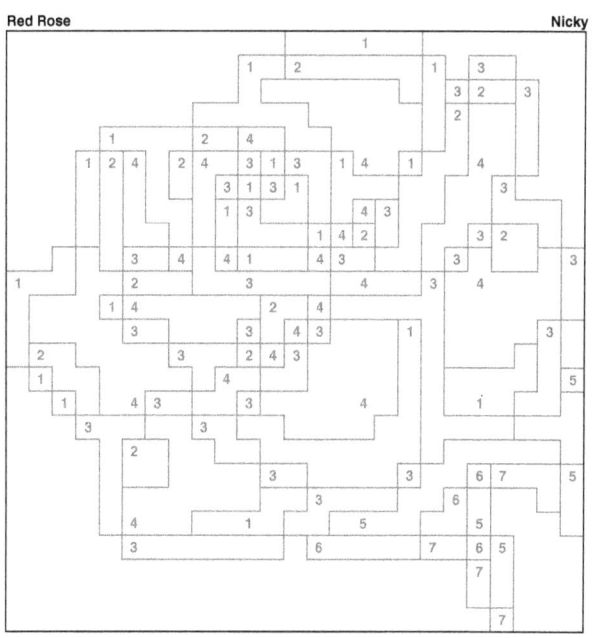

1-Jazzberry Jam, 2-Bittersweet, 3-Fuzzy Wuzzy, 4-Scarlet,
5-Outer Space, 6-Midnight Blue, 7-Blue-Green

Motorcycle — ledka

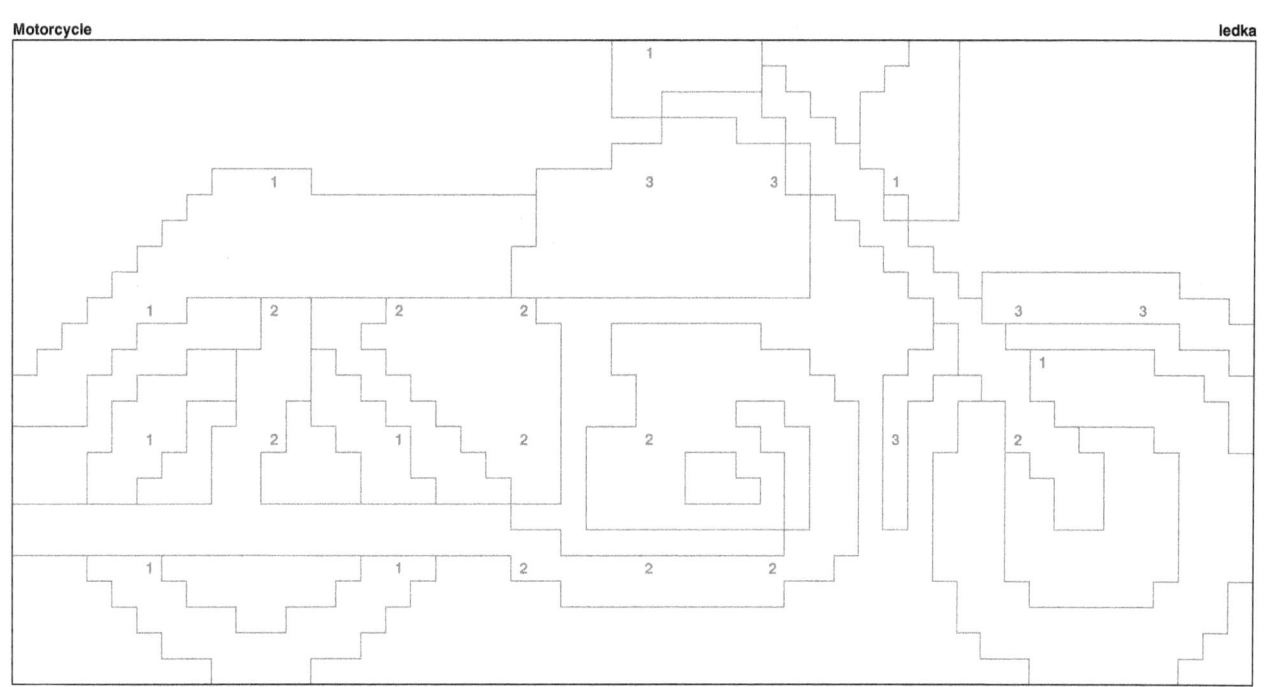

1-Black, 2-Manatee, 3-Jazzberry Jam

Alabama State Hornets　　　　　　　　　　　　　　　　　　　　　　　　　　　　　TNT

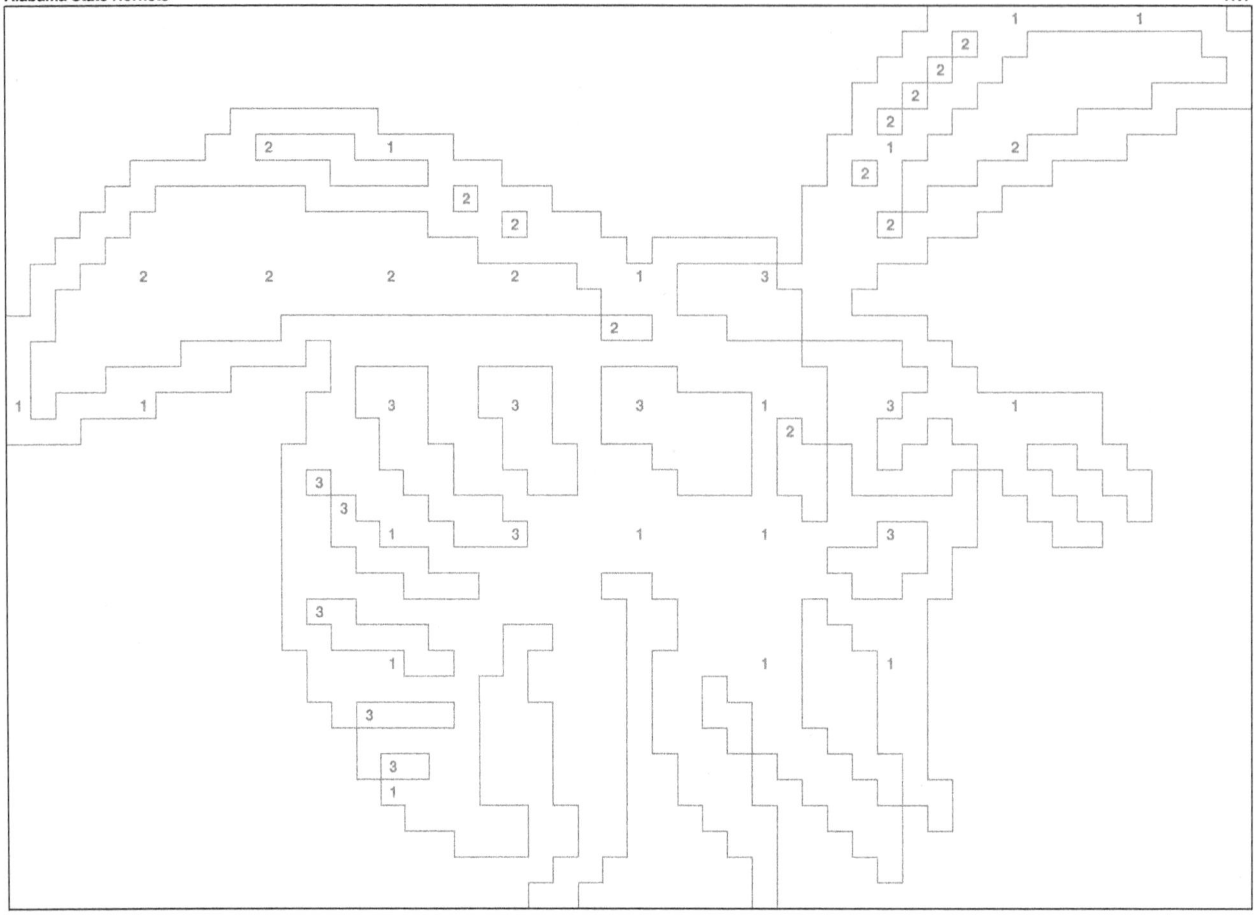

1-Black, 2-Manatee, 3-Inchworm

Let's Go!　　　　　　　　　　　　　　　　　　　　　　　　　　　　　　　　　op1

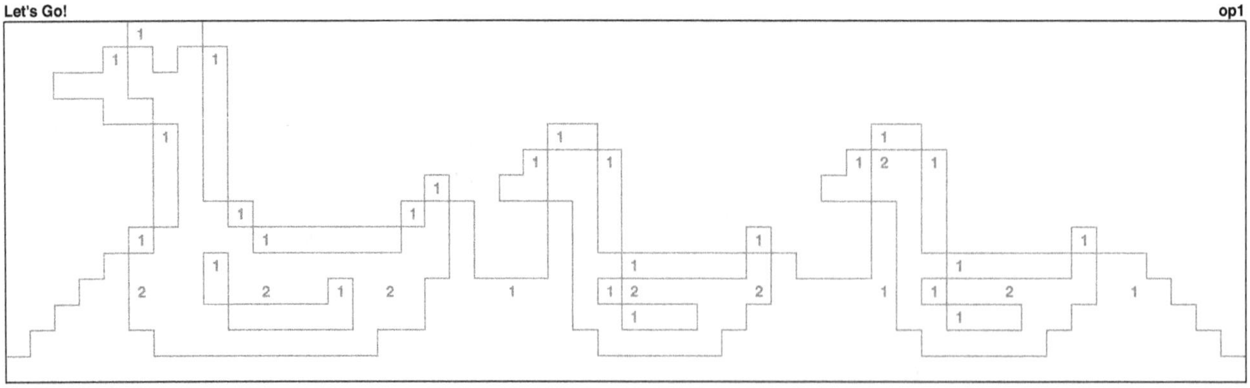

1-Black, 2-Canary

Arizona Wildcats — TNT

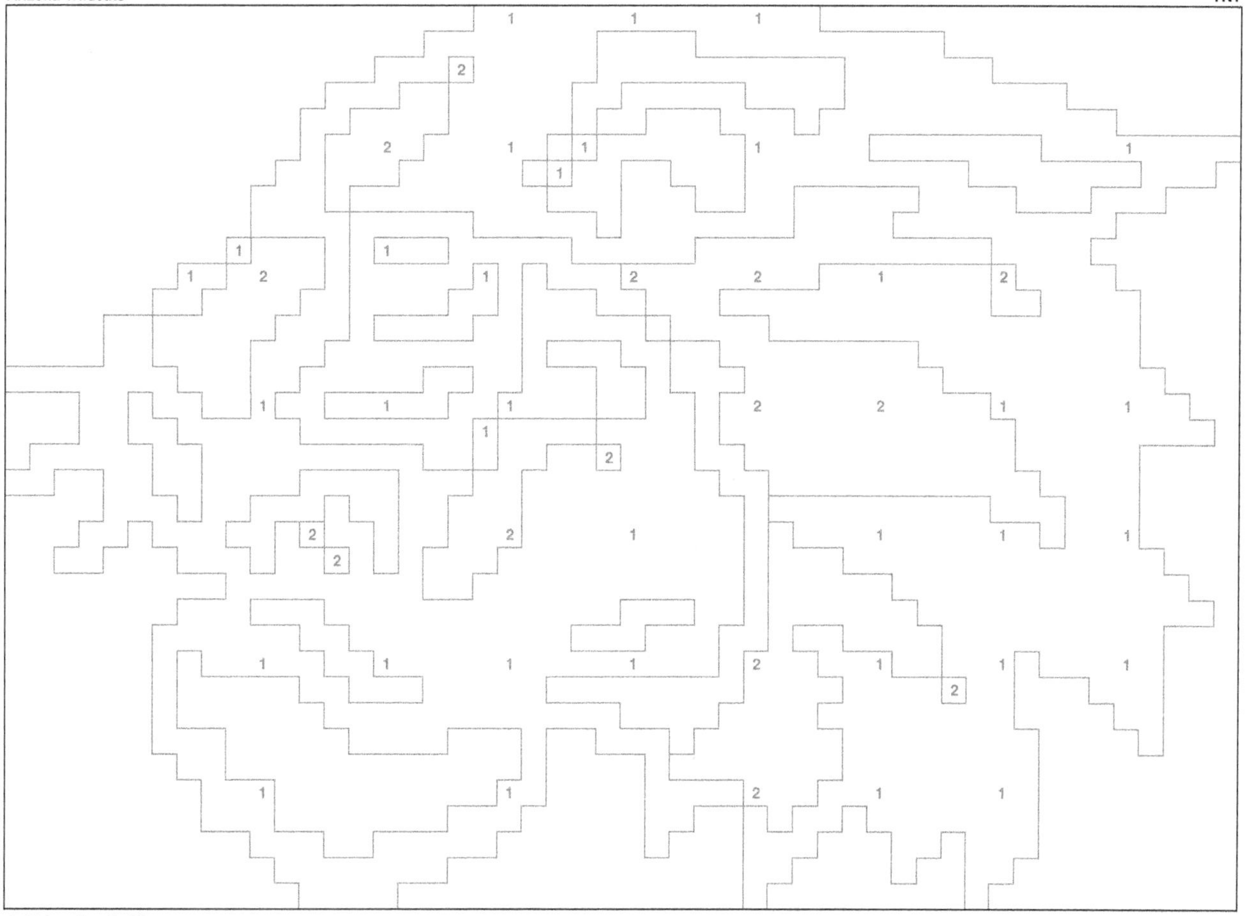

1-Black, 2-Maroon

Dragonfly — schmook1773

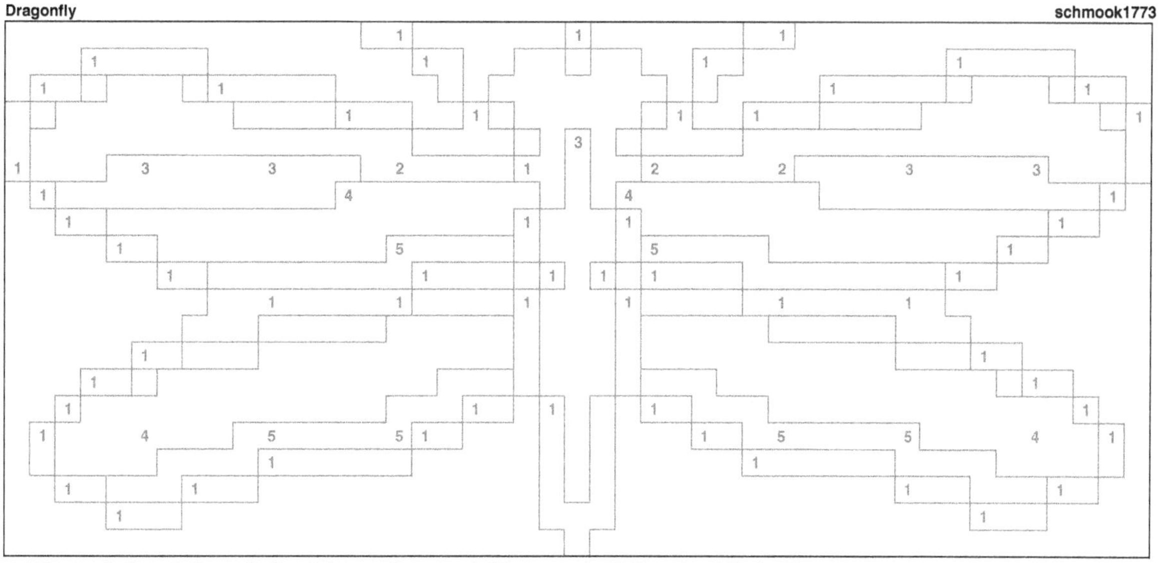

1-Black, 2-Dandelion, 3-Caribbean Green, 4-Shamrock, 5-Tropical Rain Forest

www.griddlers.net — Paint by Numbers, Vol. 1

Turtle — oren

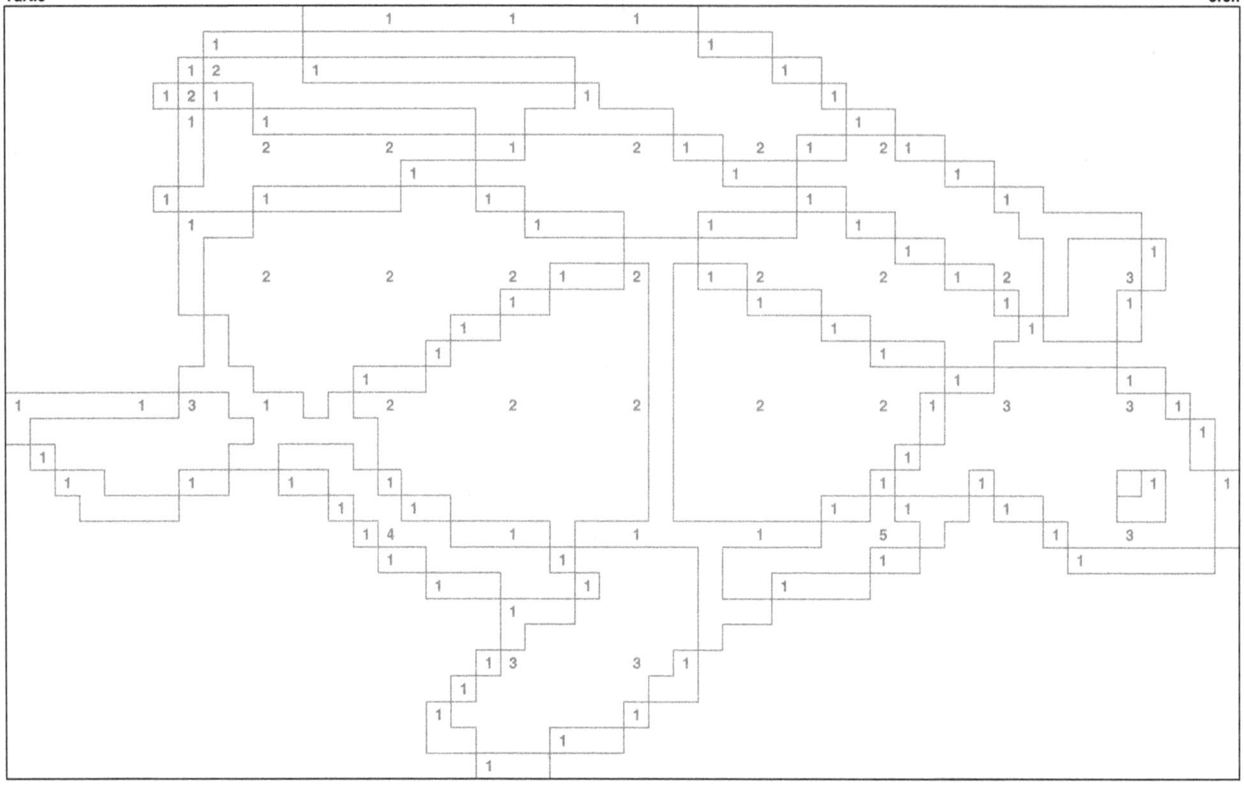

1-Black, 2-Eggplant, 3-Asparagus, 4-Tumbleweed, 5-Fuzzy Wuzzy

Camels — vtipkarjope

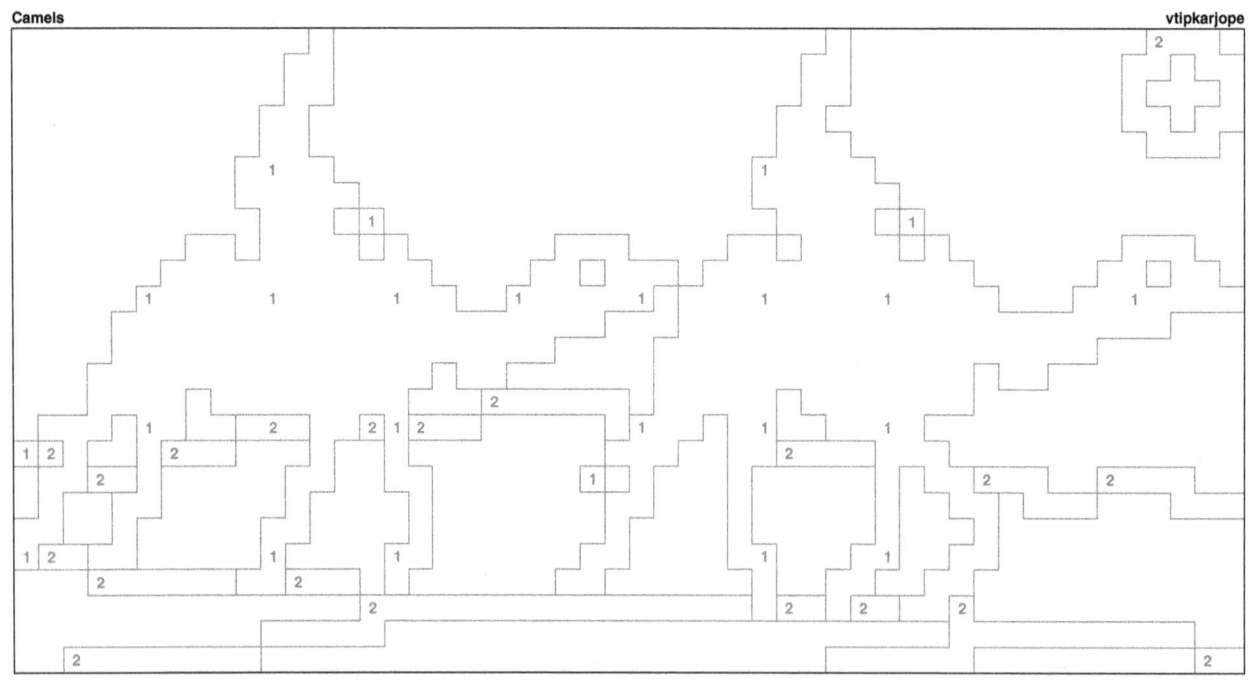

1-Black, 2-Mango Tango

Paint by Numbers, Vol. 1

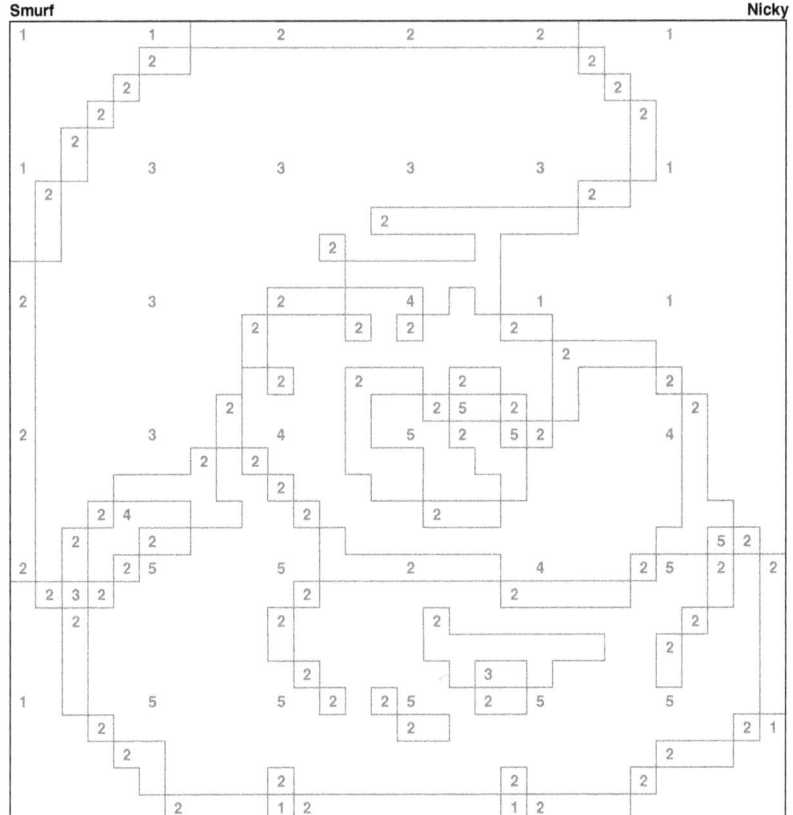

1-Inchworm, 2-Outer Space, 3-Scarlet, 4-Blue (III), 5-White

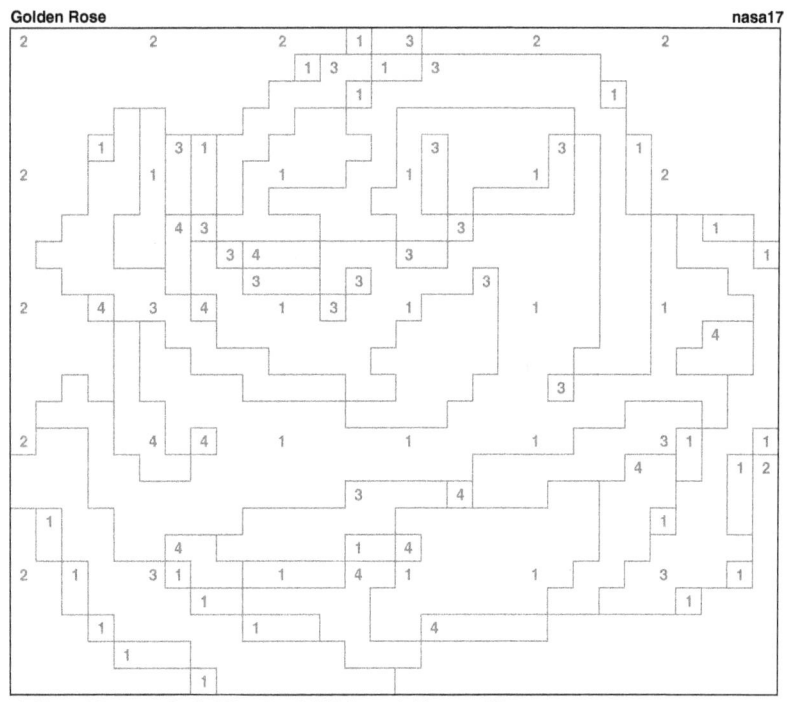

1-Tumbleweed, 2-Black, 3-White, 4-Fuzzy Wuzzy

Fruits oren

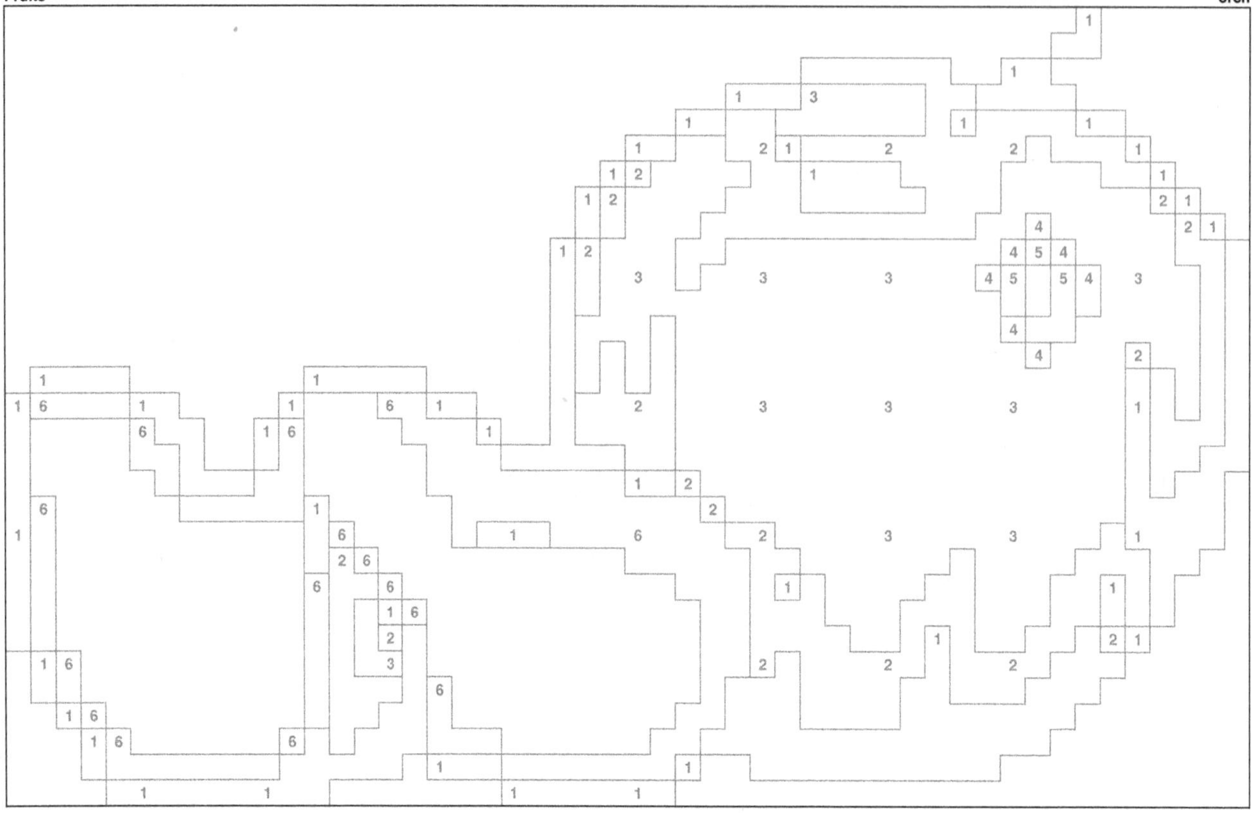

1-Black, 2-Maroon, 3-Scarlet, 4-Carnation Pink, 5-Pig Pink, 6-Canary

Hedgehog MagdalenaAlb

1-Black, 2-White, 3-Mahogany

Cow — oren

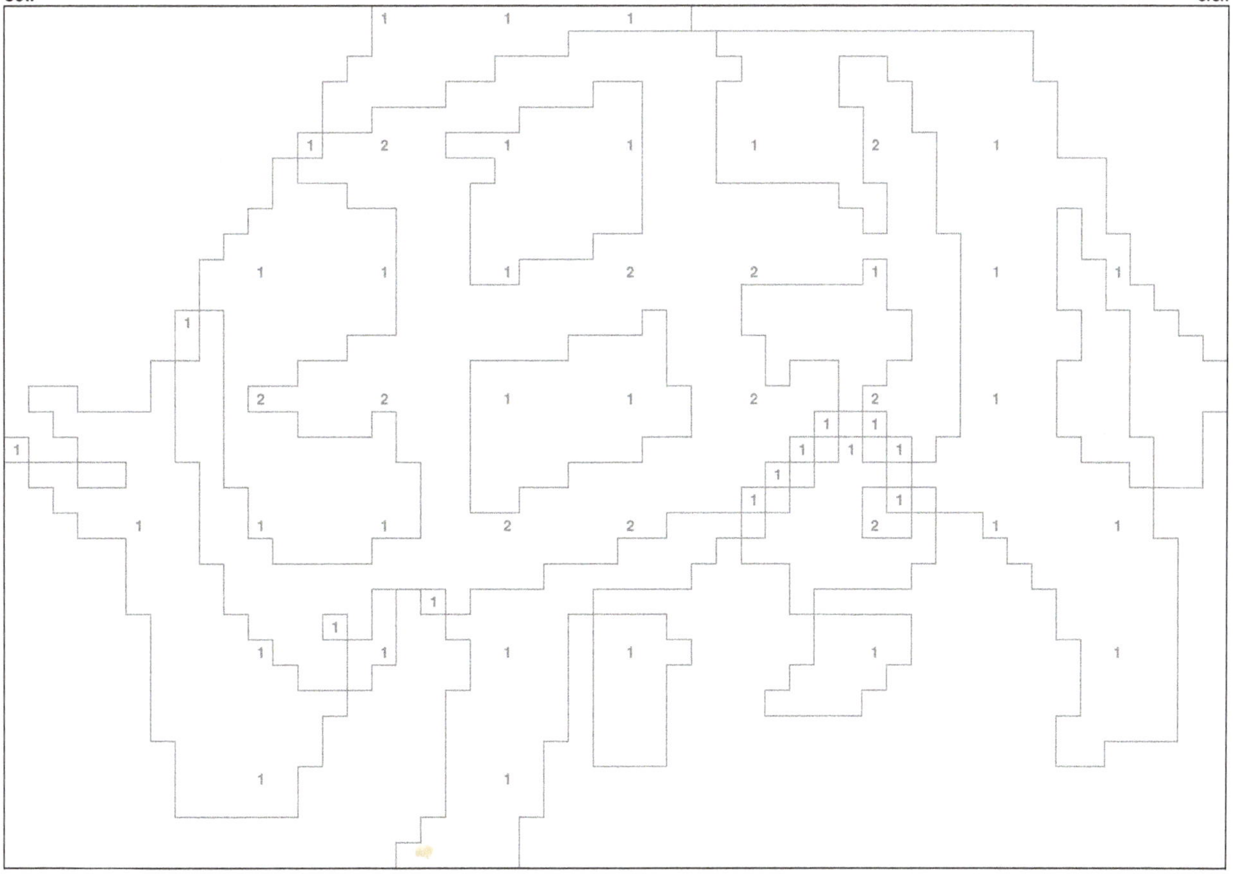

1-Outer Space, 2-Orange

Begging — abrek

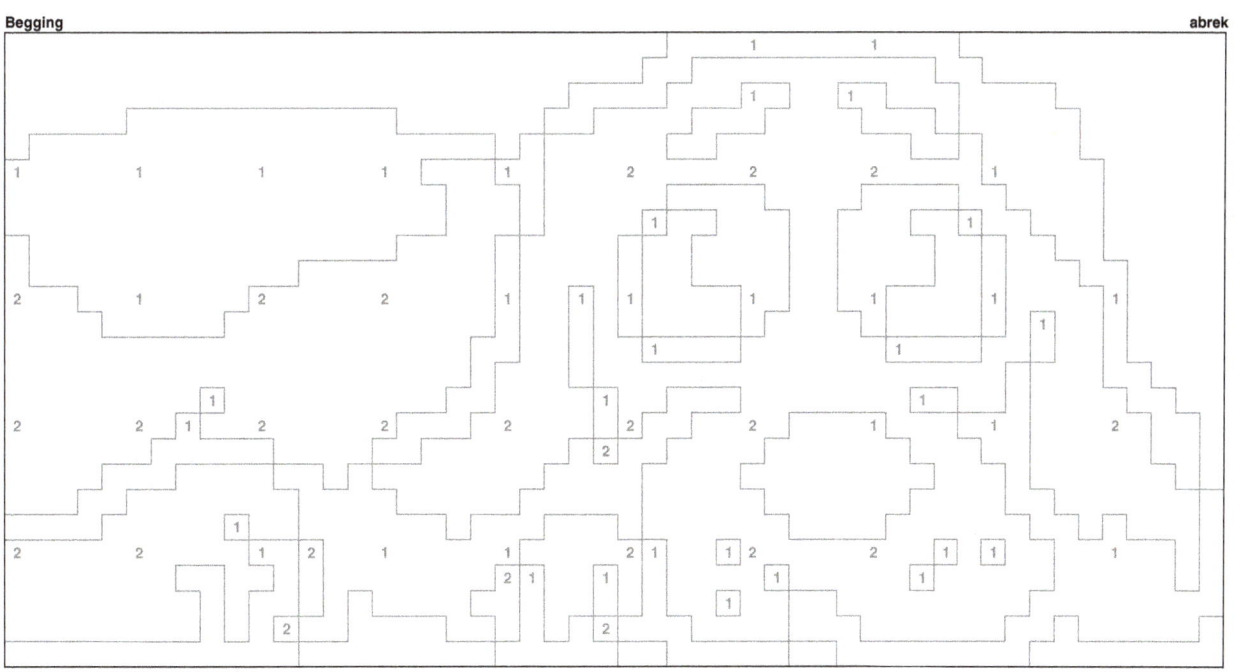

1-Black, 2-Pig Pink

Bread — oren

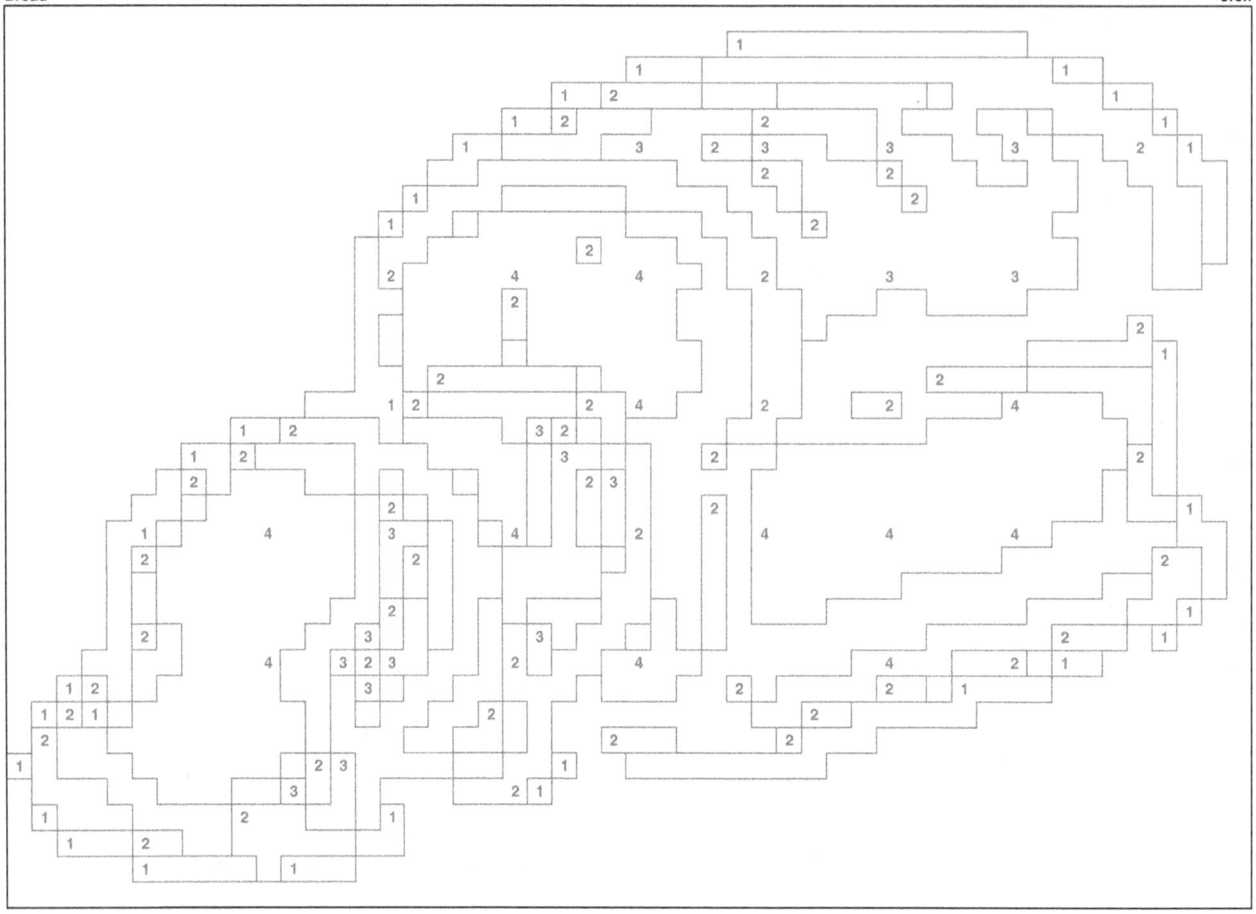

1-Tan, 2-Black, 3-Goldenrod, 4-Apricot

Bomberman — animgirl

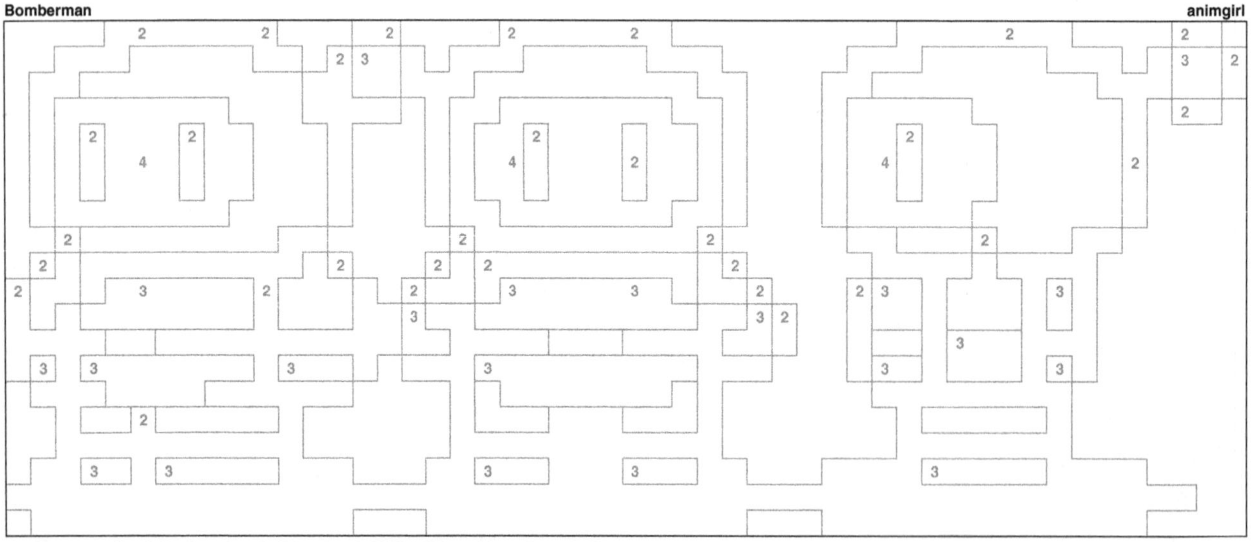

1-Granny Smith Apple, 2-Black, 3-Wild Blue Yonder, 4-Orange

Maryland Terrapins   TNT

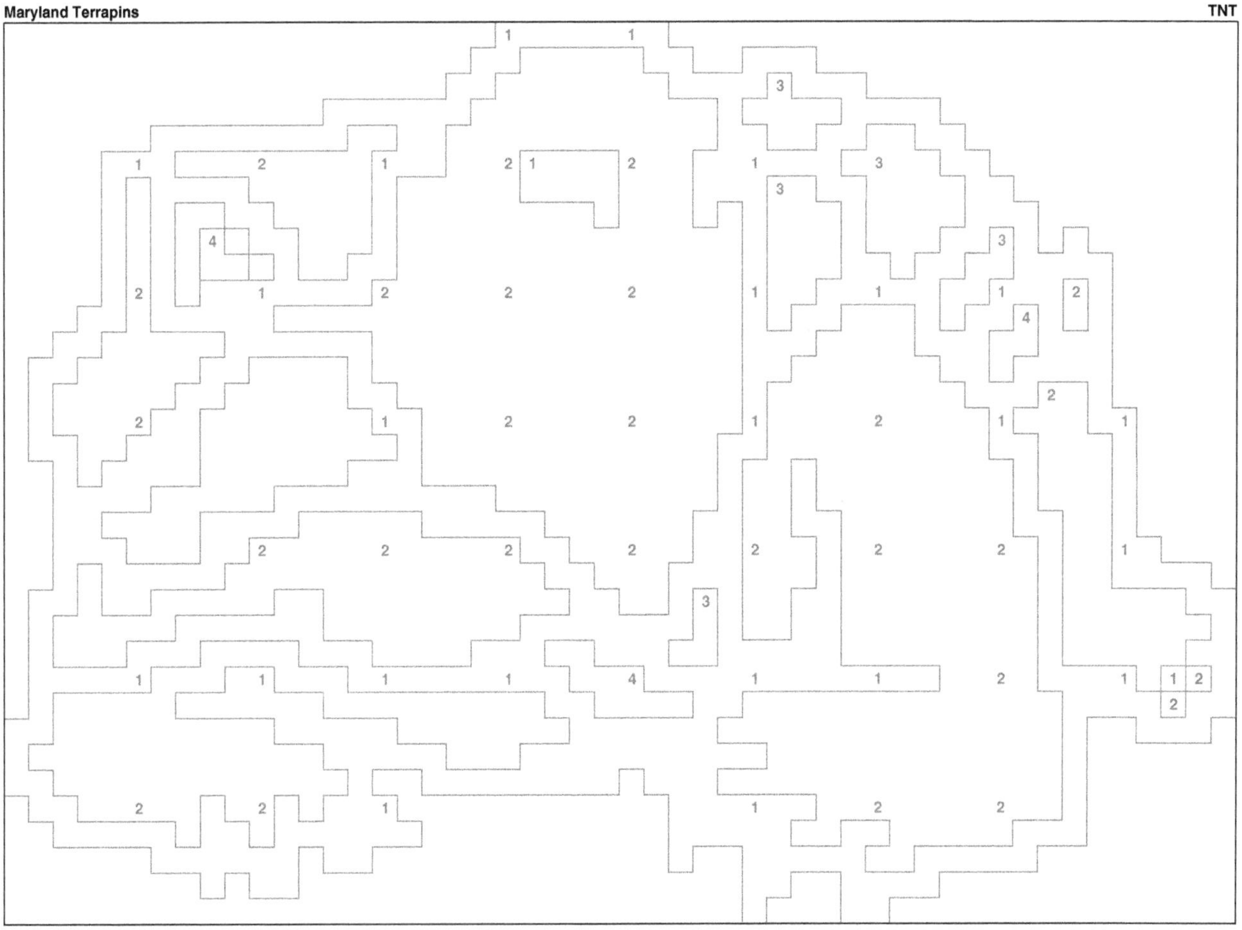

1-Black, 2-Olive Green, 3-Maroon, 4-Yellow-Orange

1924 Bugatti '35'   f1comp

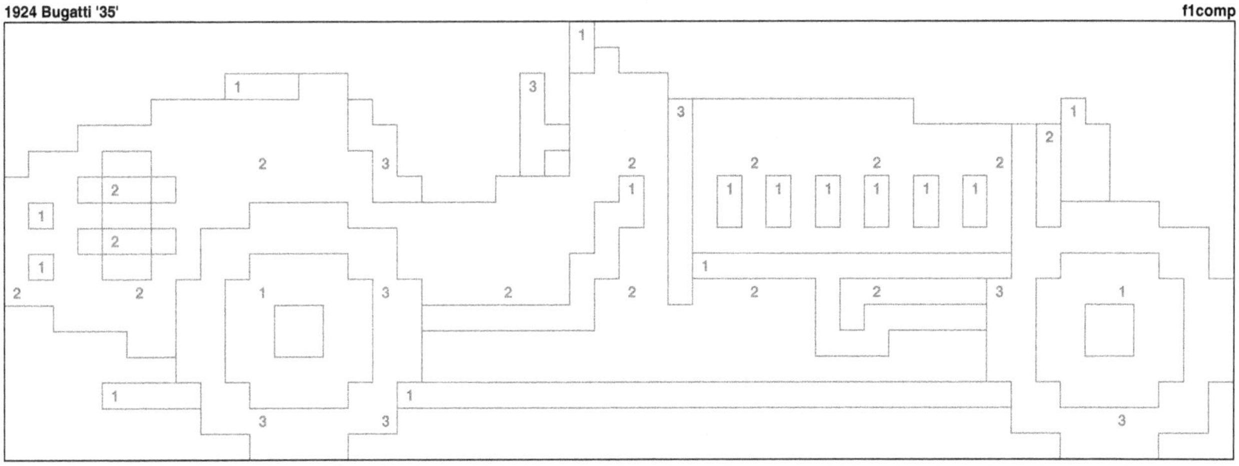

1-Periwinkle, 2-Blue-Green, 3-Black

Red Squirrel — bombastico

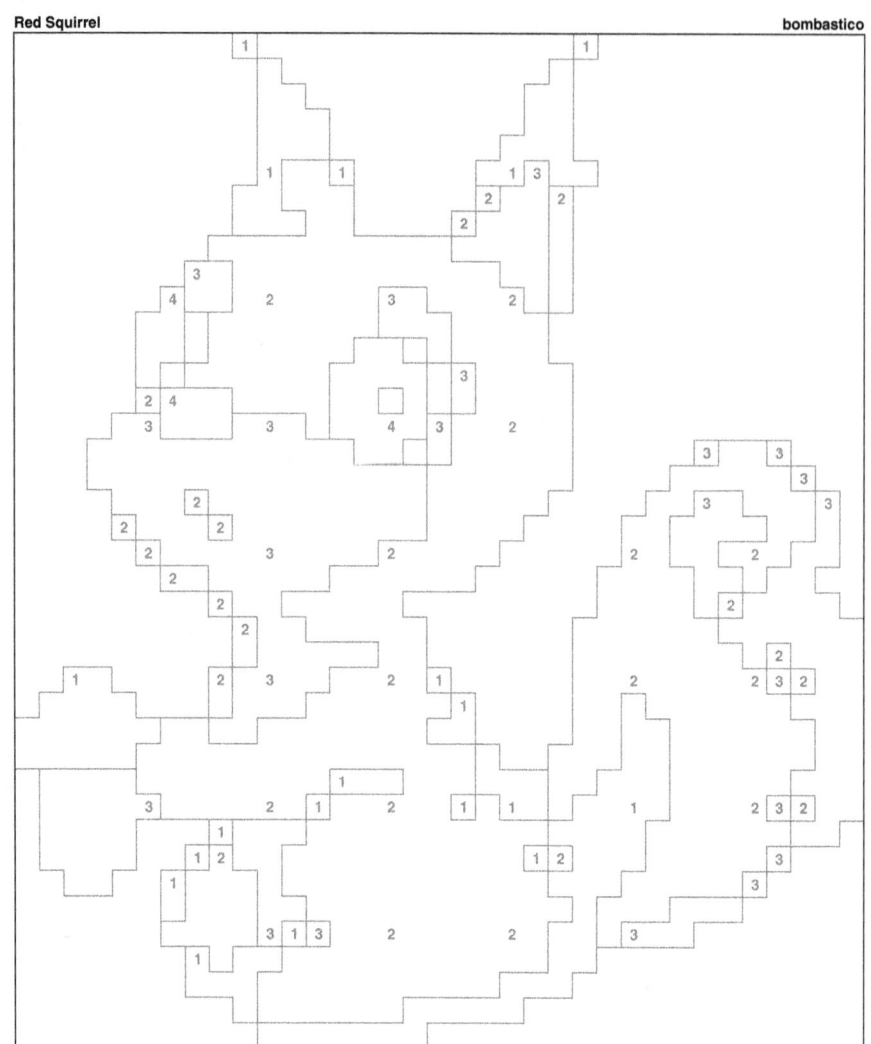

1-Fuzzy Wuzzy, 2-Mahogany, 3-Timberwolf, 4-Black

Sunglasses — elimaor

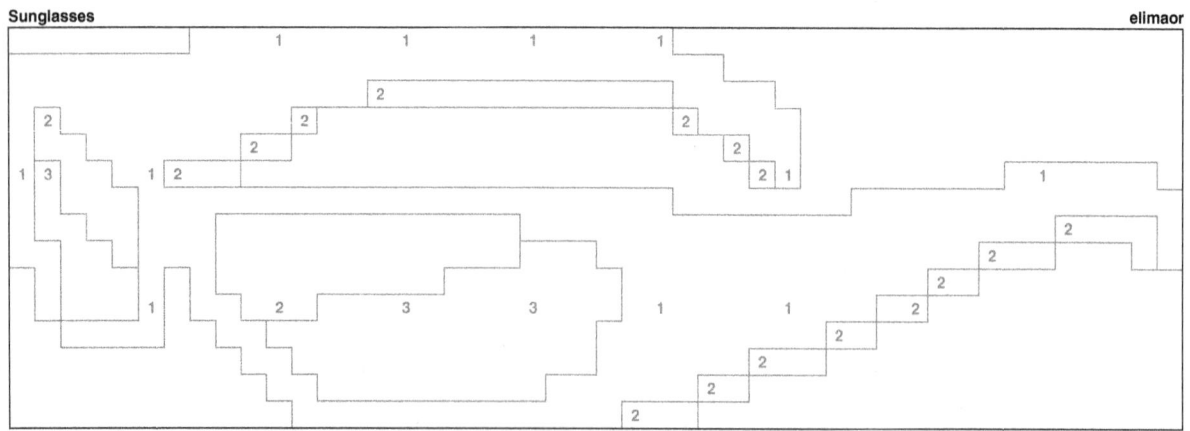

1-Fuzzy Wuzzy, 2-Timberwolf, 3-Blue Bell

Florida Gators TNT

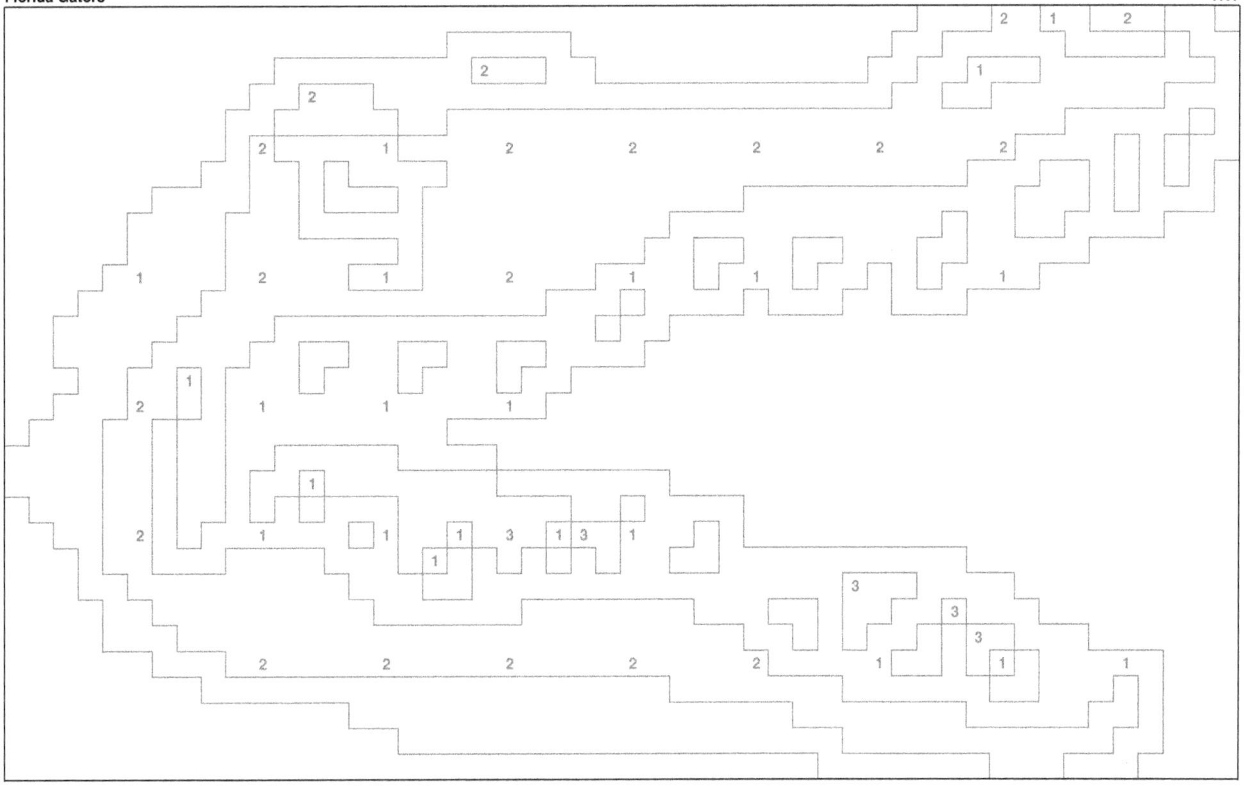

1-Black, 2-Tropical Rain Forest, 3-Red-Orange

Flowers aga0211p

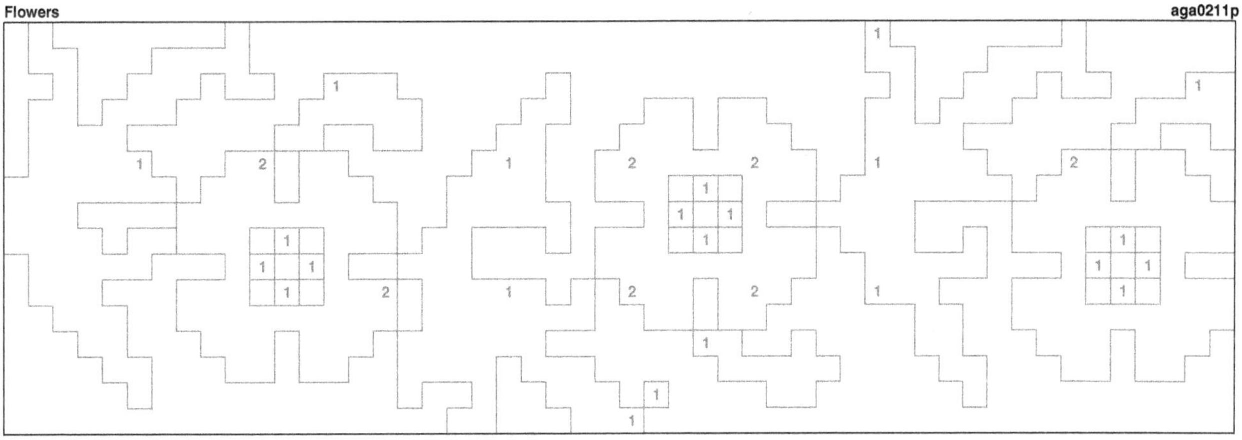

1-Black, 2-Denim

Kentucky Wildcats **TNT**

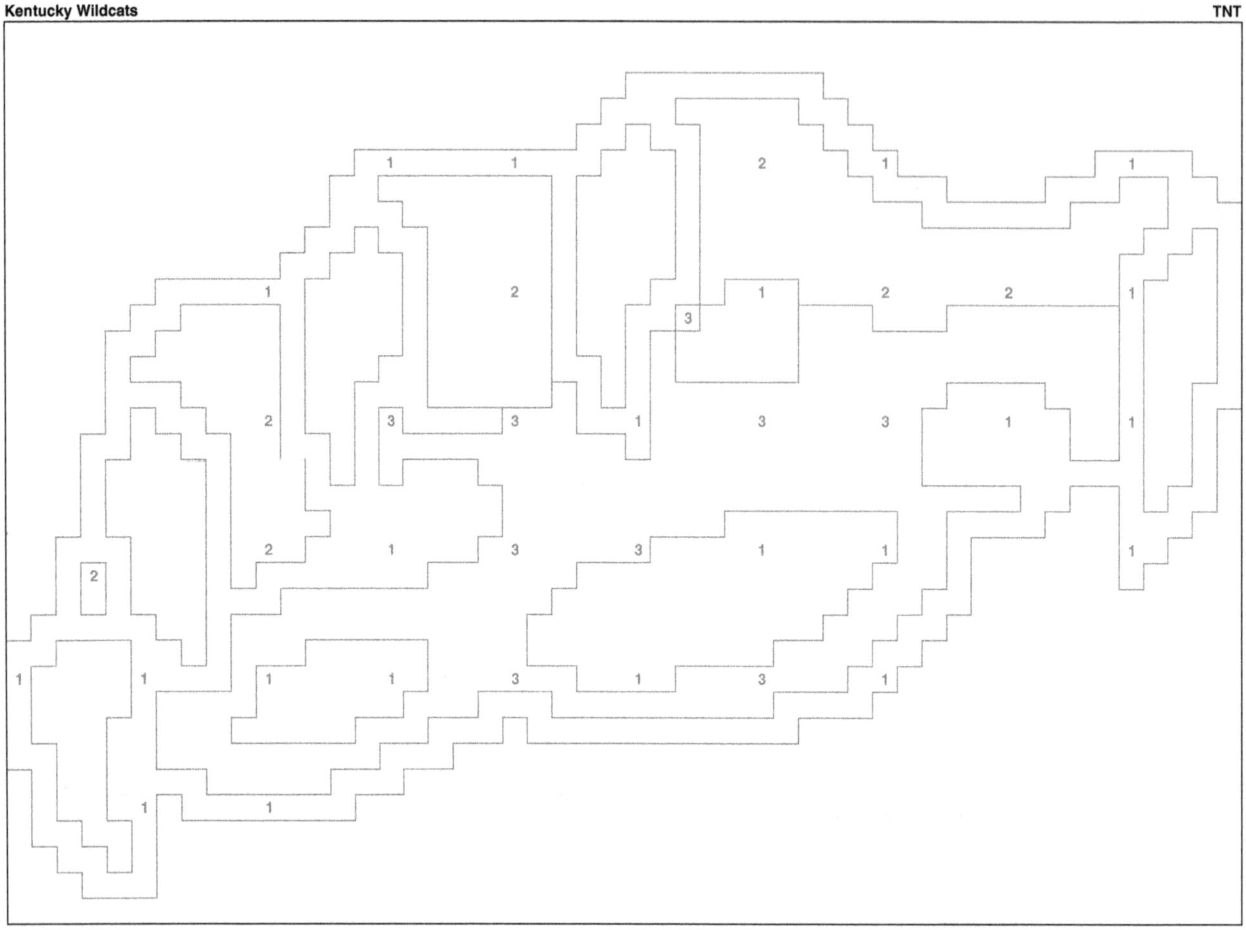

1-Black, 2-Yellow-Orange, 3-Beaver

Penguins **abrek**

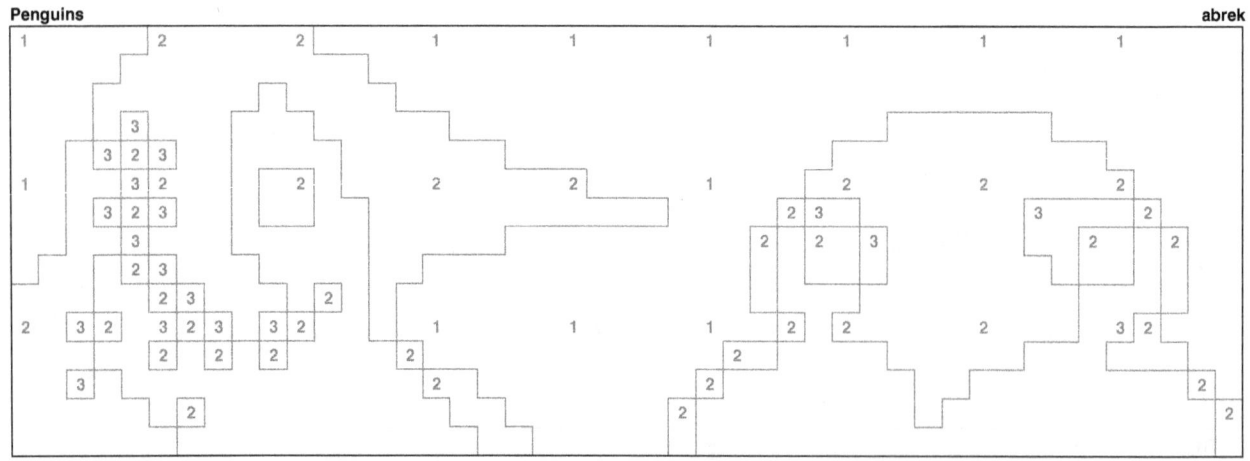

1-Periwinkle, 2-Black, 3-White

Florida International Golden Panther — TNT

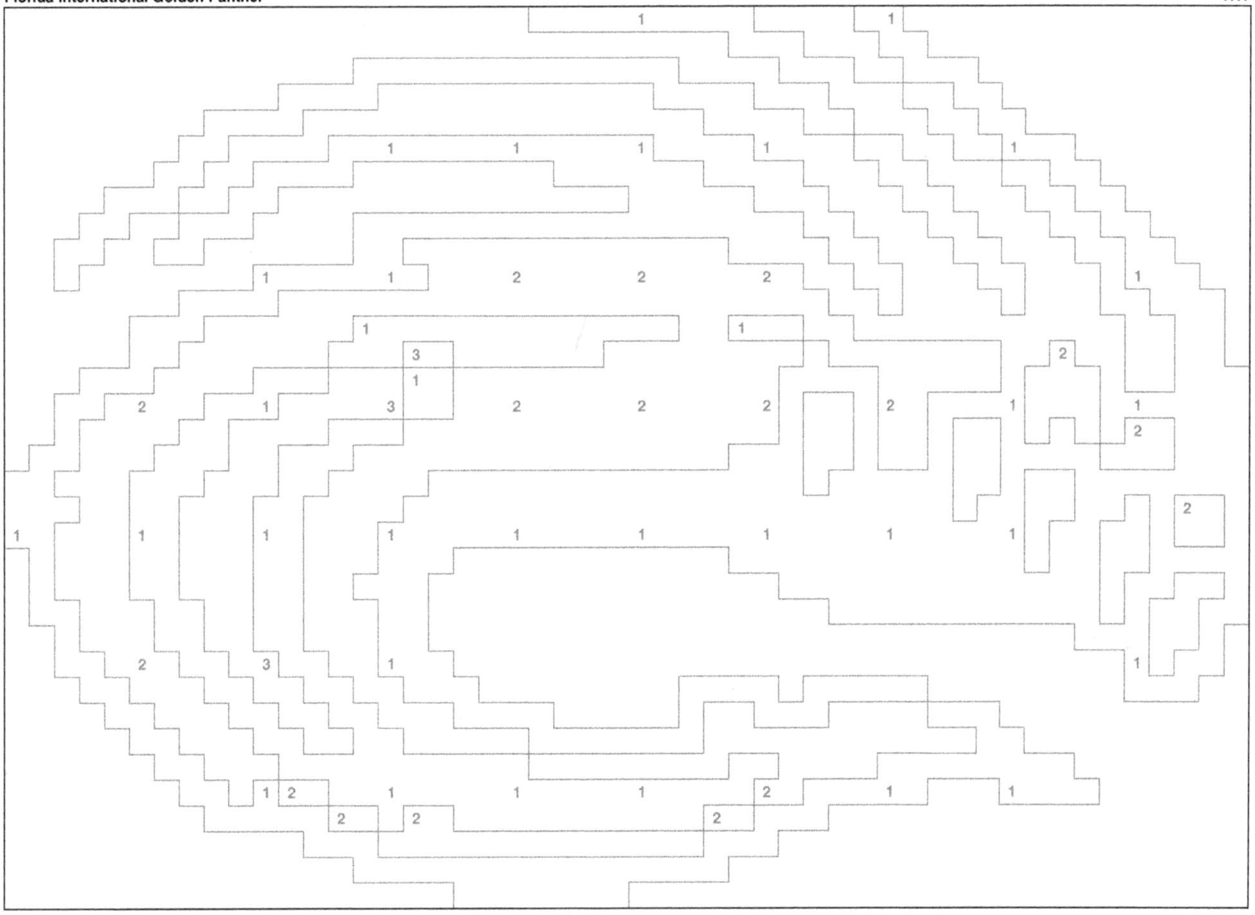

1-Midnight Blue, 2-Dandelion, 3-Jazzberry Jam

Toy Train — Nicky

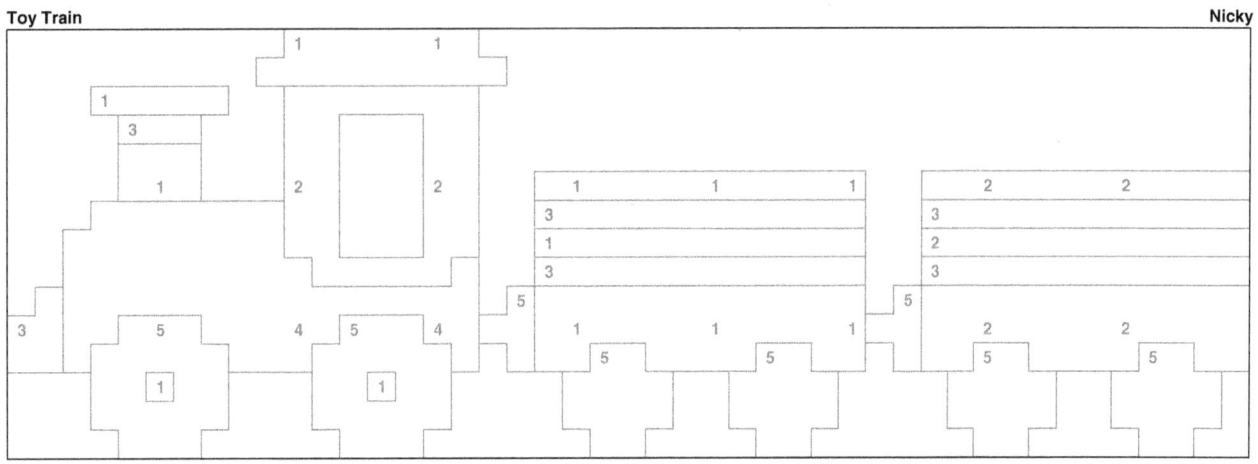

1-Dandelion, 2-Midnight Blue, 3-Jazzberry Jam, 4-Cerulean Blue, 5-Black

Dolphin — Nicky

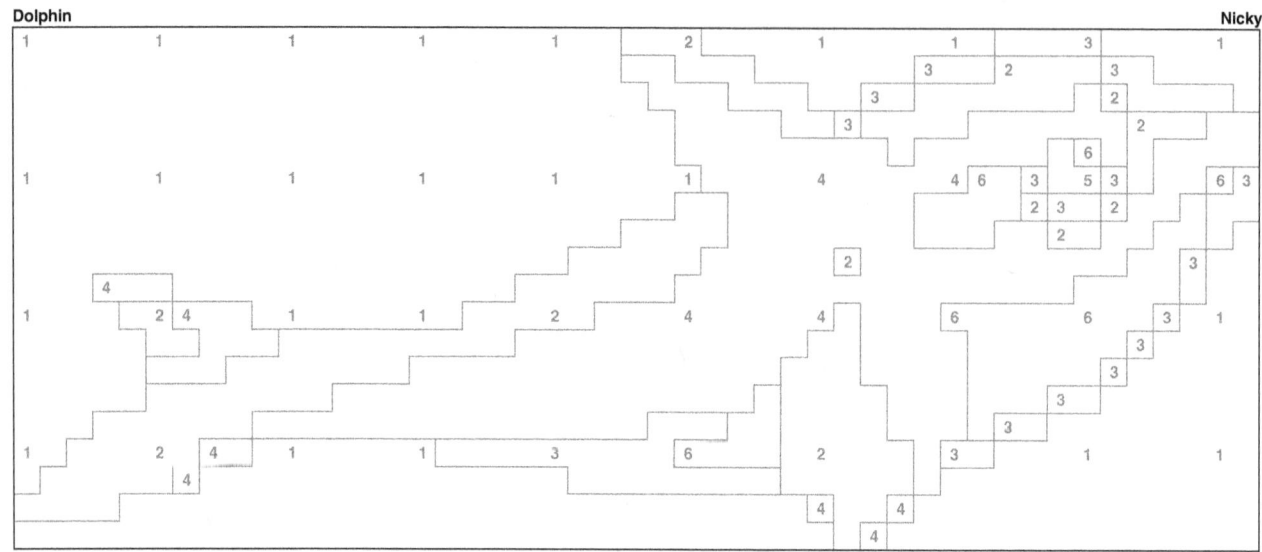

1-Yellow-Green, 2-Blue Bell, 3-Periwinkle, 4-Royal Purple, 5-Black, 6-White

Bat Attack — arcadedweller

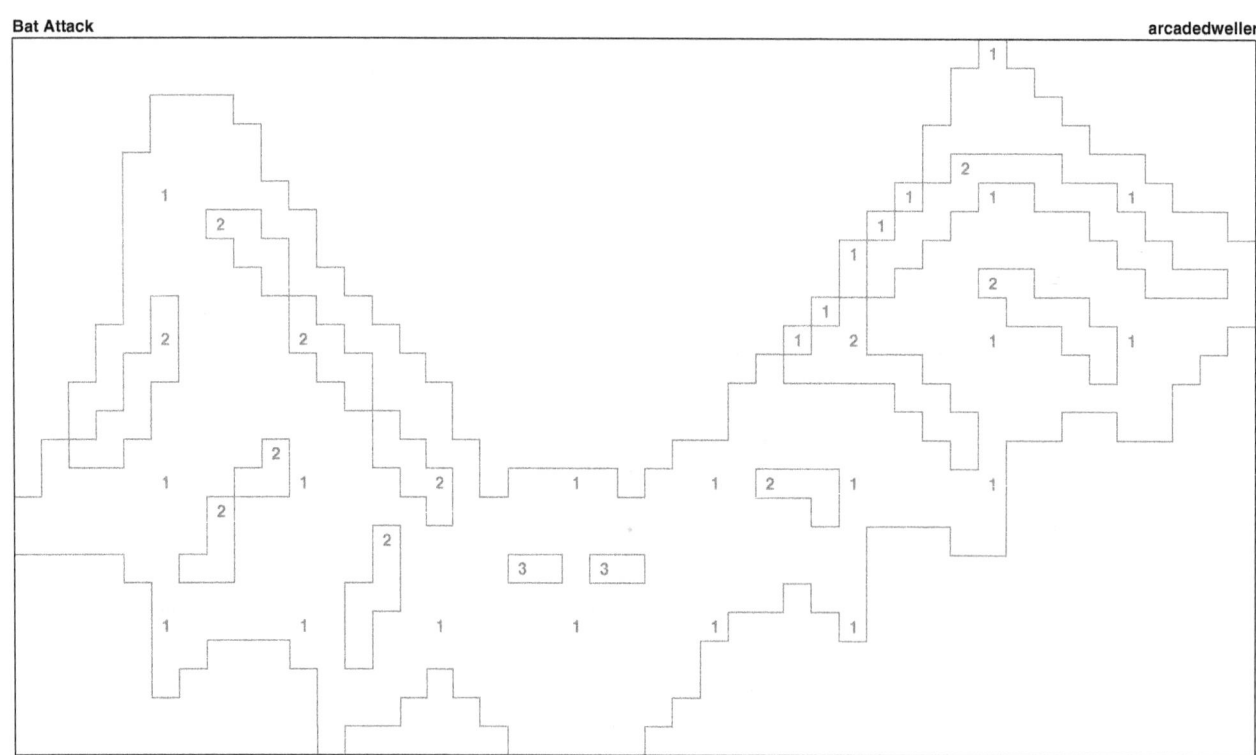

1-Black, 2-Manatee, 3-Scarlet

Ducks — ulka

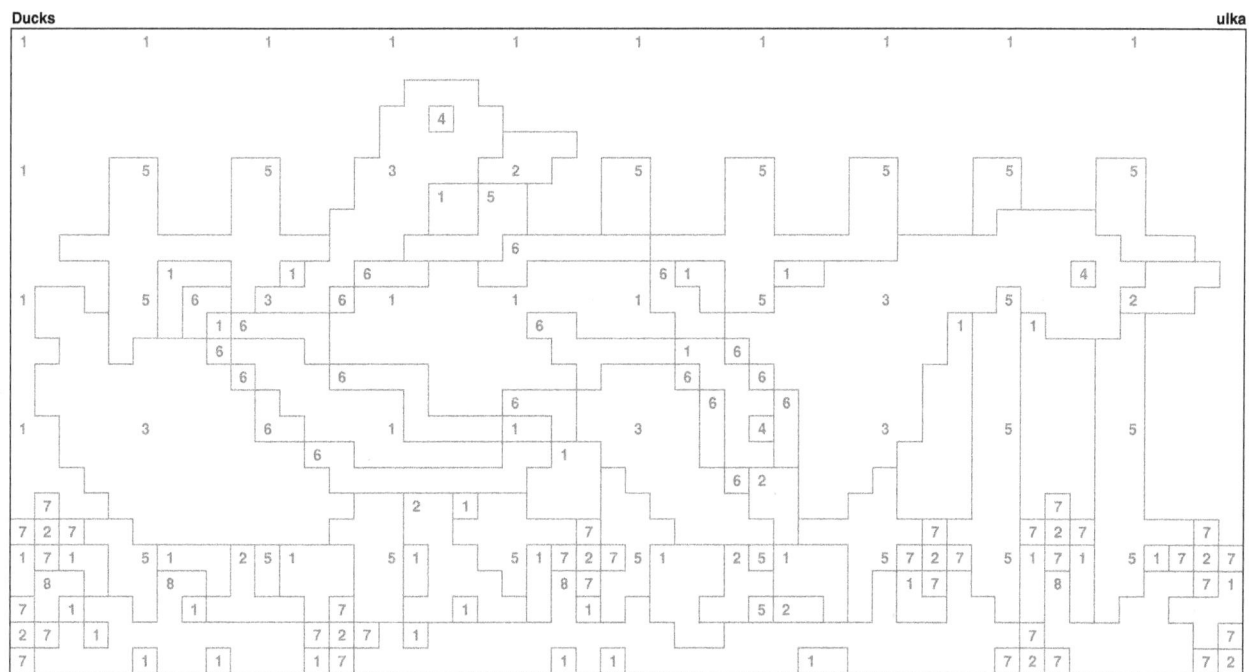

1-White, 2-Red-Orange, 3-Banana Mania, 4-Black, 5-Tumbleweed, 6-Cadet Blue, 7-Yellow-Orange, 8-Granny Smith Apple

Swordfish — Nicky

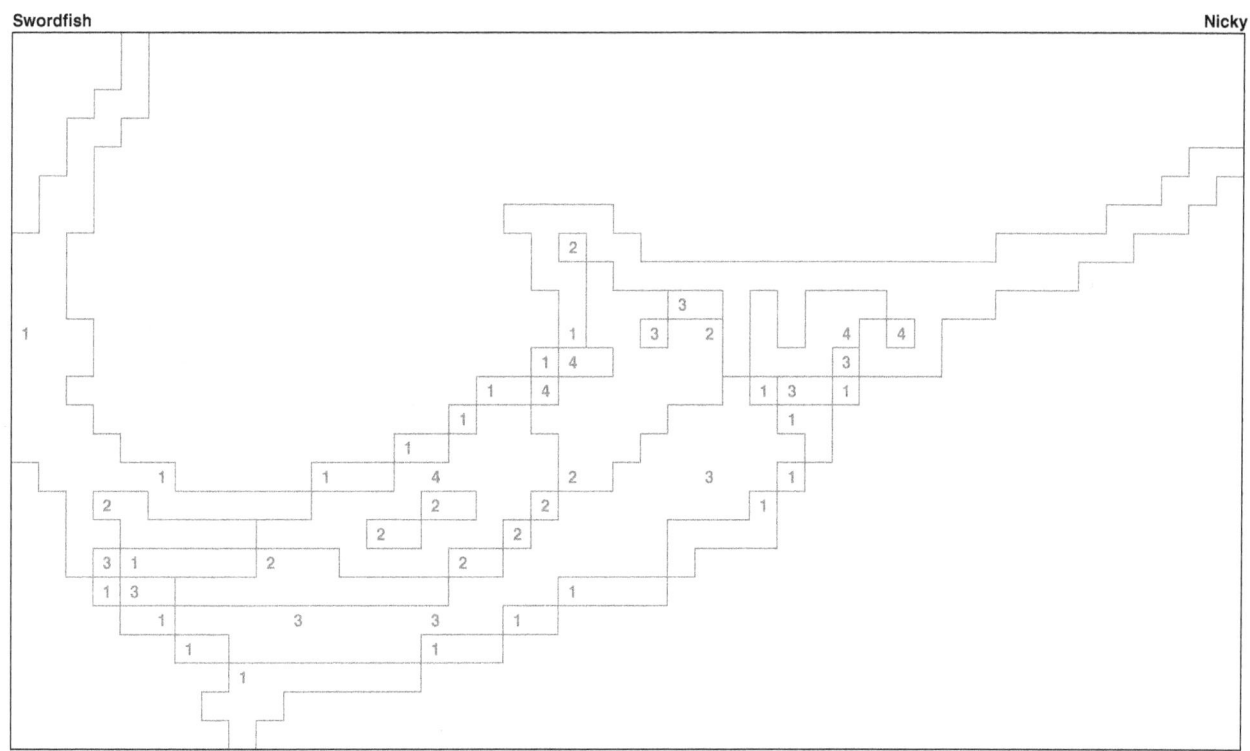

1-Black, 2-Midnight Blue, 3-Aquamarine, 4-Denim

Roses are Red

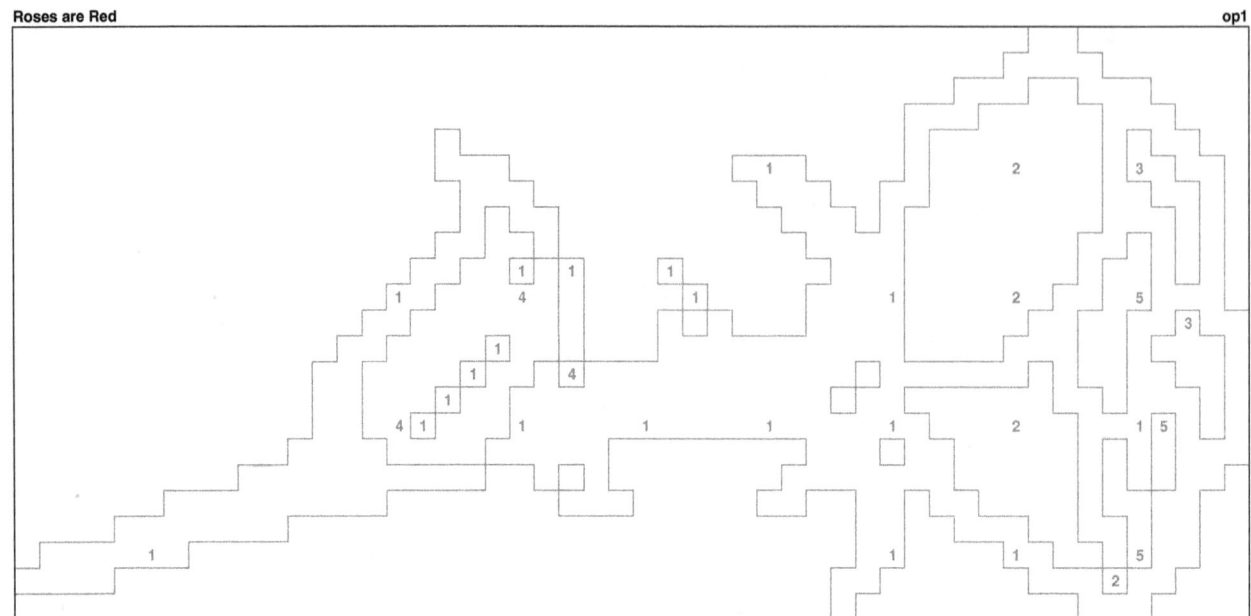

1-Black, 2-Jazzberry Jam, 3-Salmon, 4-Fern, 5-Scarlet

Trumpet

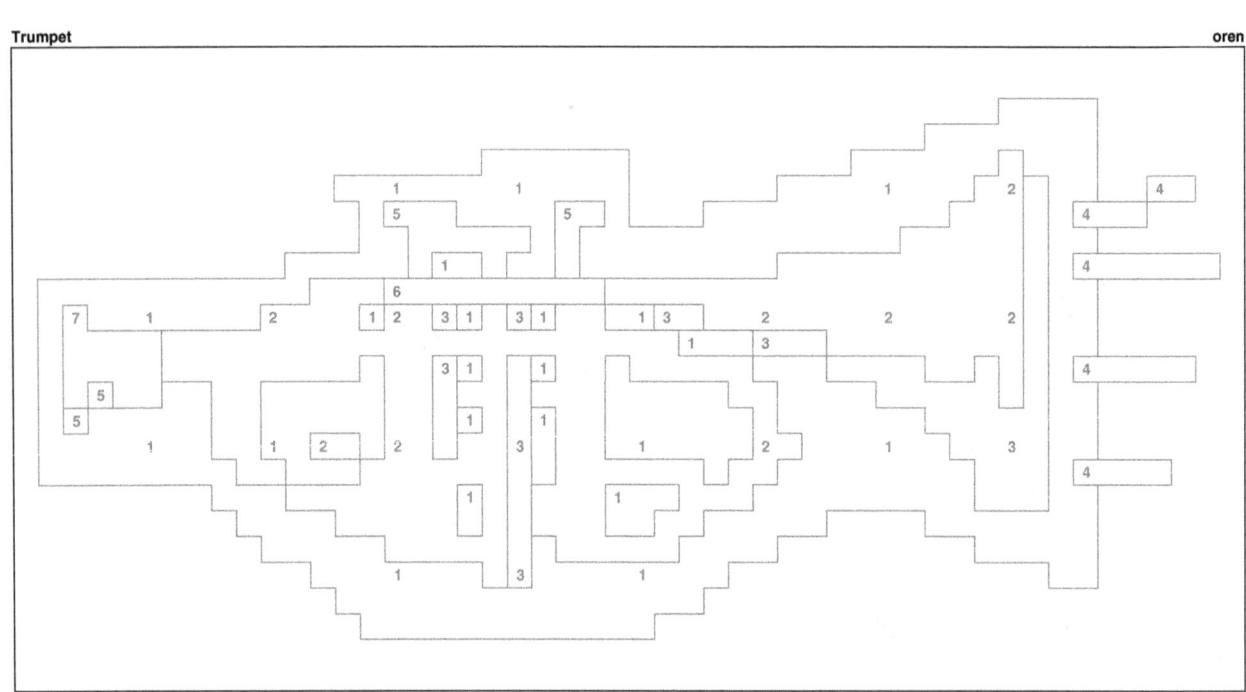

1-Black, 2-Yellow-Orange, 3-Mango Tango, 4-Periwinkle, 5-Cadet Blue, 6-Dandelion, 7-Timberwolf

Doggie — **Nicky**

1-Wild Blue Yonder, 2-Timberwolf, 3-Desert Sand, 4-Tan, 5-Pig Pink, 6-Eggplant, 7-Brown, 8-Manatee

Happy Shroom   **Nicky**

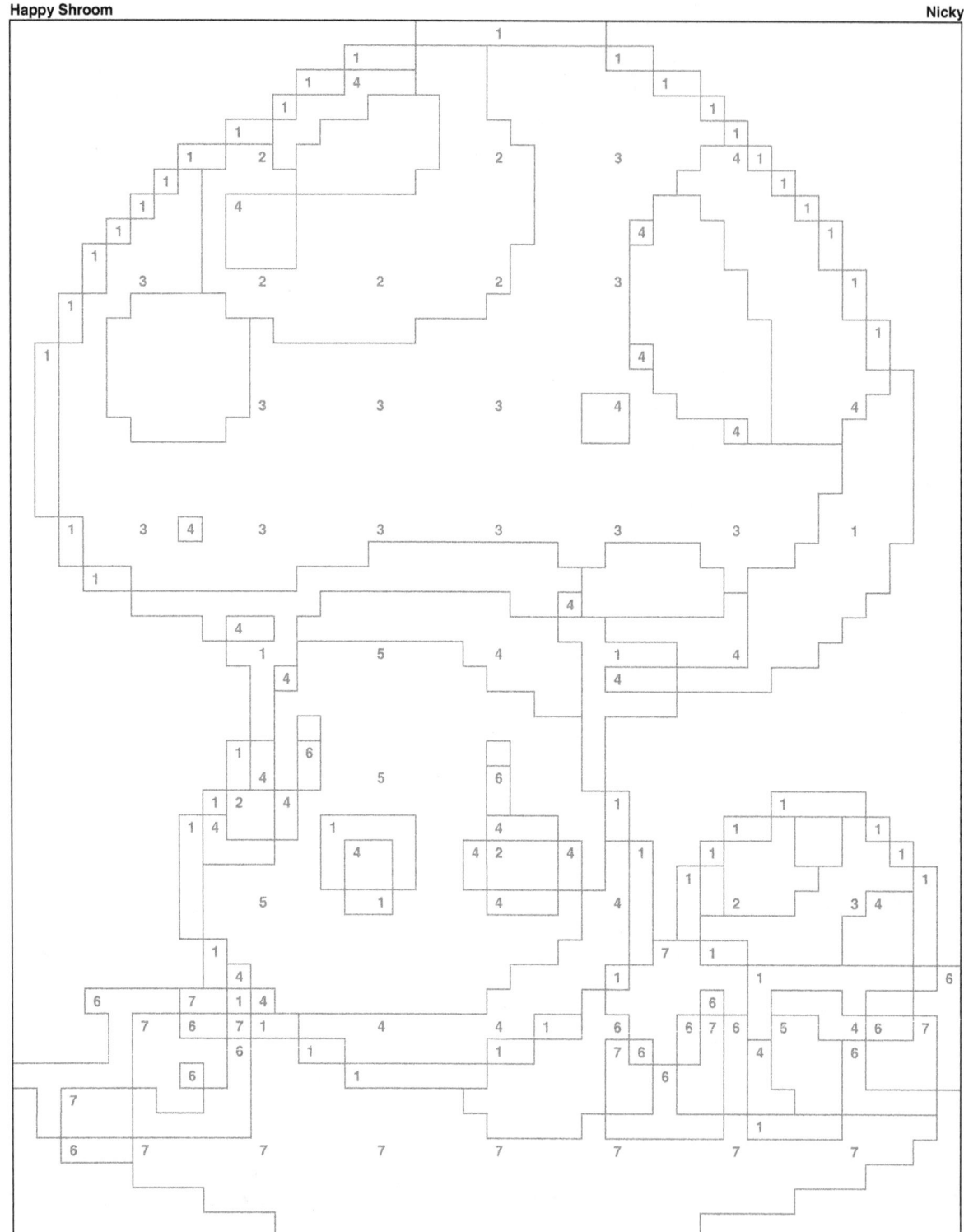

1-Jazzberry Jam, 2-Bittersweet, 3-Sunset Orange, 4-Peach, 5-Canary, 6-Green, 7-Inchworm

Dalmatian

1-Black, 2-Timberwolf, 3-Indian Red, 4-Tan

Lou Jacobs (Ringling Bros Clown) popkin

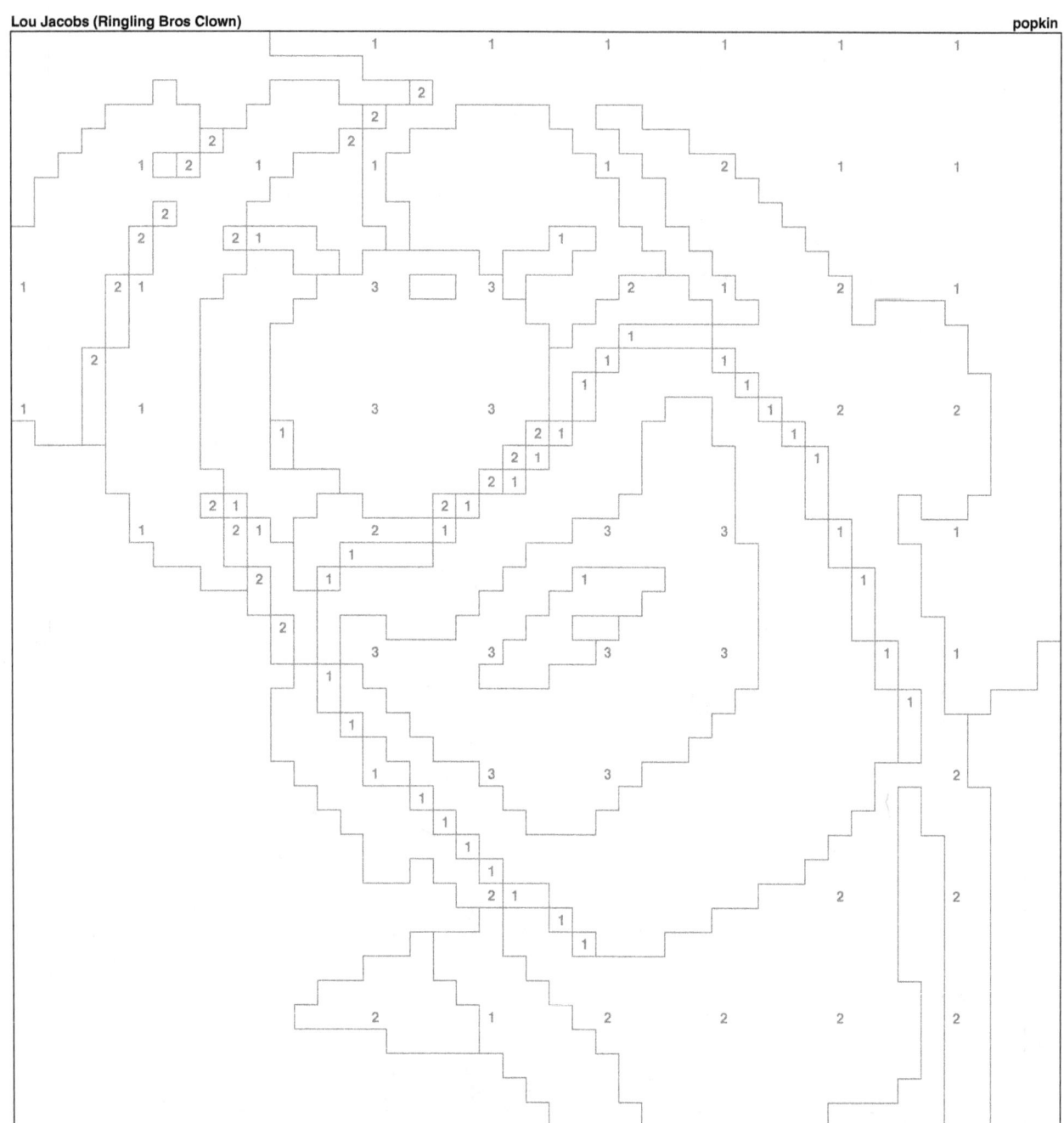

1-Black, 2-Timberwolf, 3-Scarlet

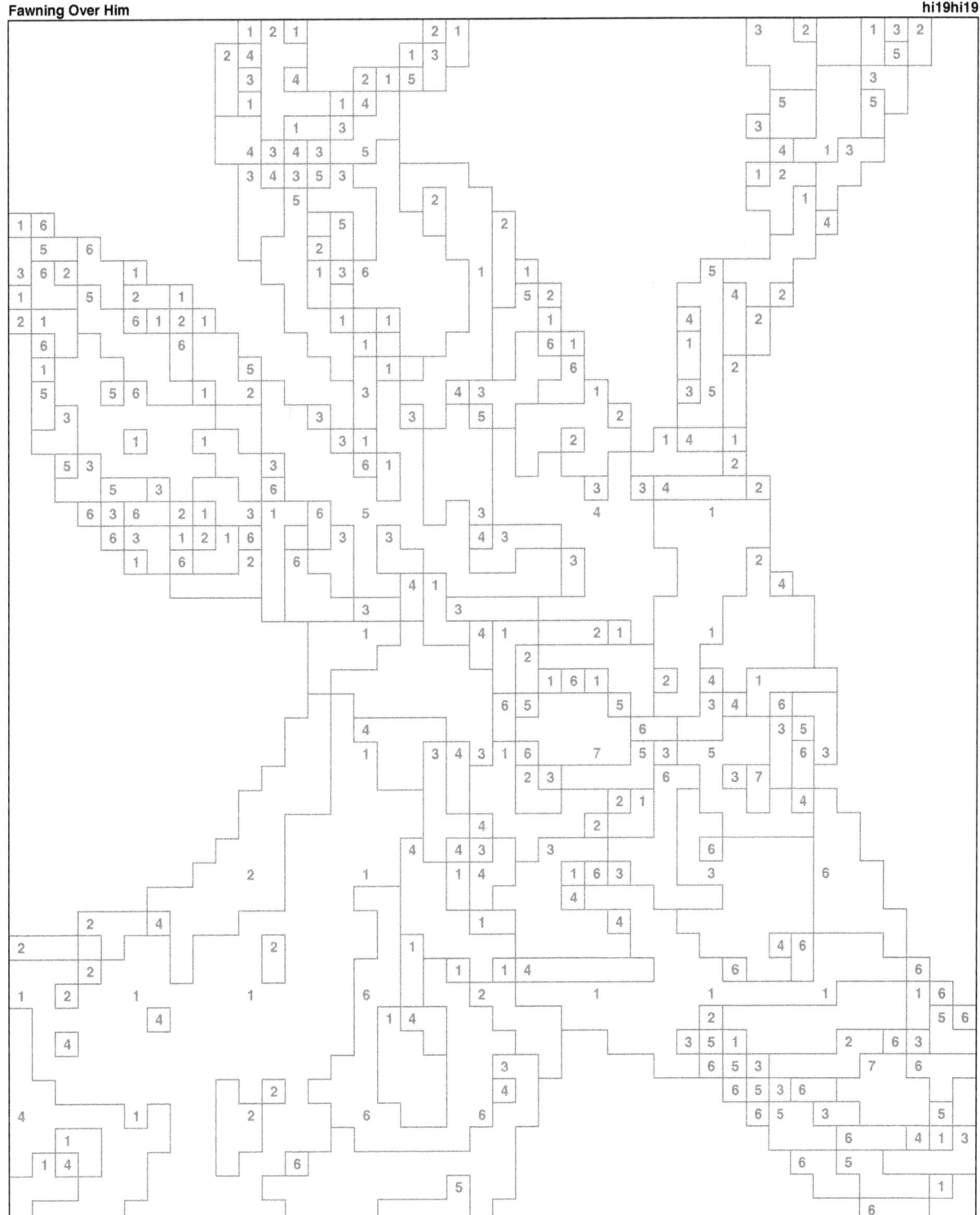

Wizard of Oz - Wicked Witch — Glucklich

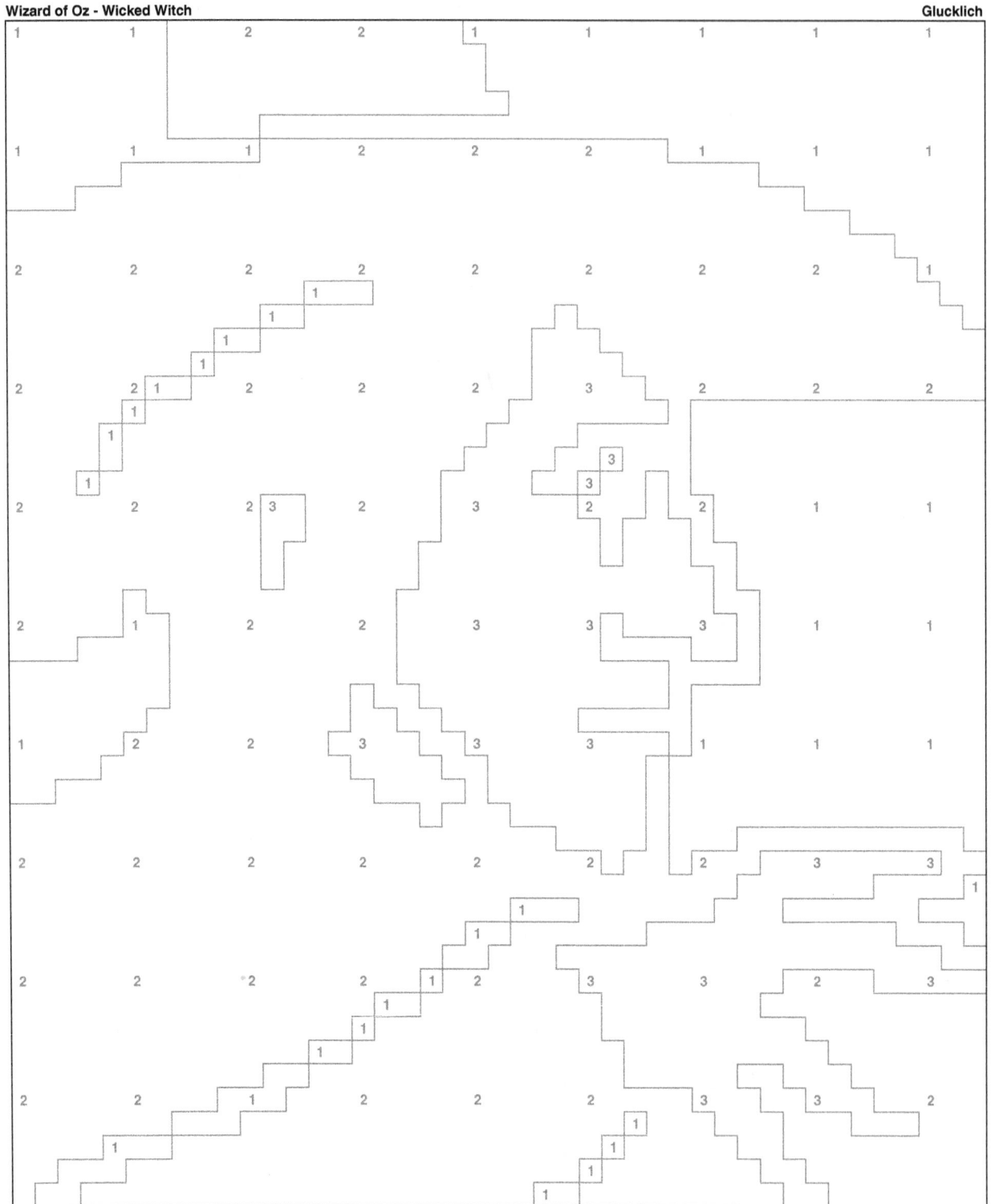

1-Manatee, 2-Black, 3-Granny Smith Apple

1-Tumbleweed, 2-Raw Sienna, 3-Timberwolf, 4-Black

Brigitte Bardot mudshark

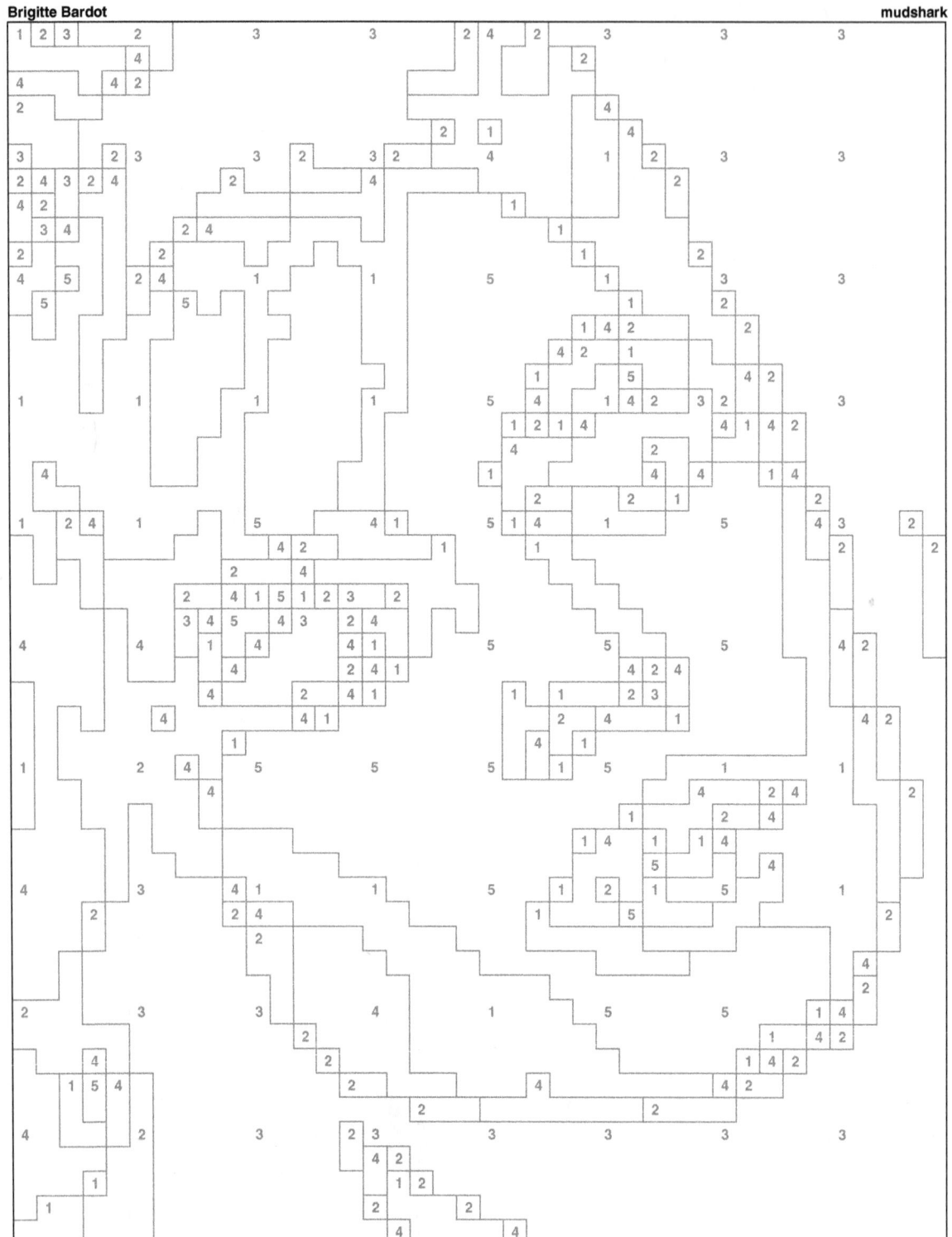

1-Cadet Blue, 2-Outer Space, 3-Black, 4-Manatee, 5-White

Farfetch'd - Pokemon No. 083

1-Black, 2-Shadow, 3-Tropical Rain Forest, 4-Spring Green, 5-Green, 6-Yellow-Green, 7-Yellow-Orange

Monty Burns — bart88

1-Outer Space, 2-Dandelion, 3-Manatee, 4-Green, 5-Salmon

Lady Amherst's Pheasant — Glucklich

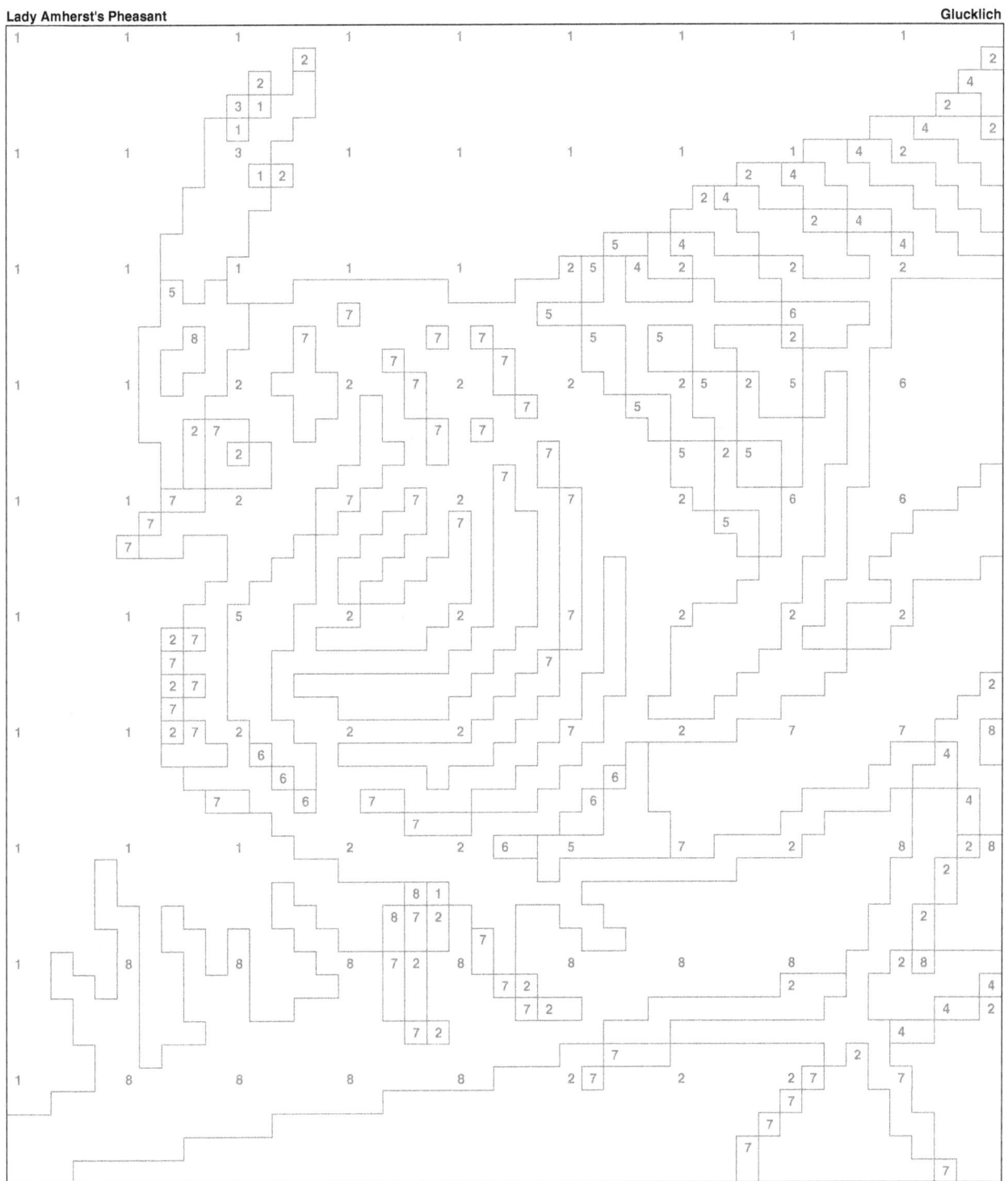

1-Tumbleweed, 2-Black, 3-Mahogany, 4-Mango Tango, 5-Tropical Rain Forest, 6-Midnight Blue, 7-Spring Green, 8-Shadow

Beautiful and Colorful — Joopie

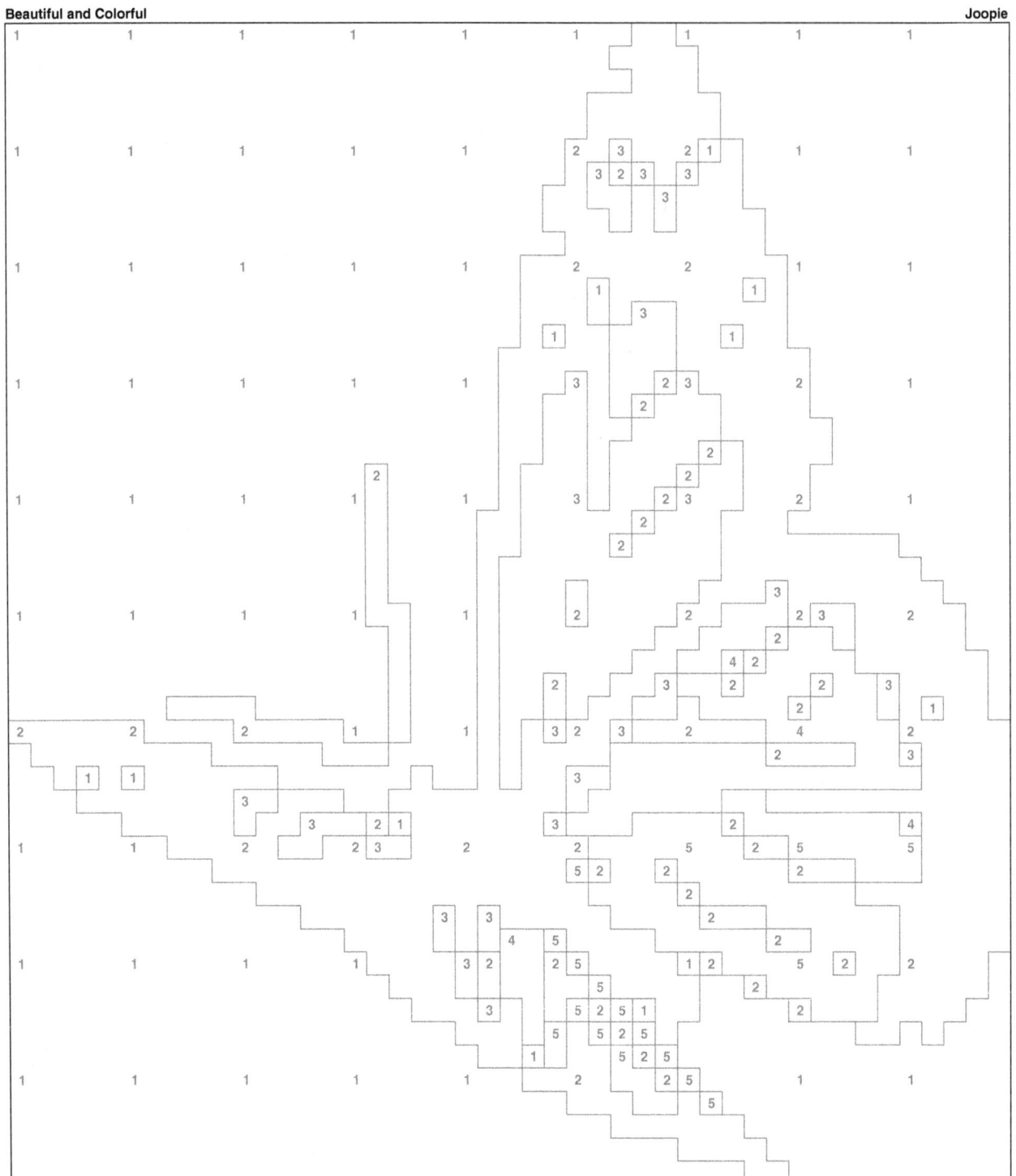

1-White, 2-Outer Space, 3-Yellow-Orange, 4-Macaroni and Cheese, 5-Banana Mania

Redhead stumpy

1-Tan, 2-Indian Red, 3-Fuzzy Wuzzy, 4-Outer Space, 5-Desert Sand, 6-Royal Purple

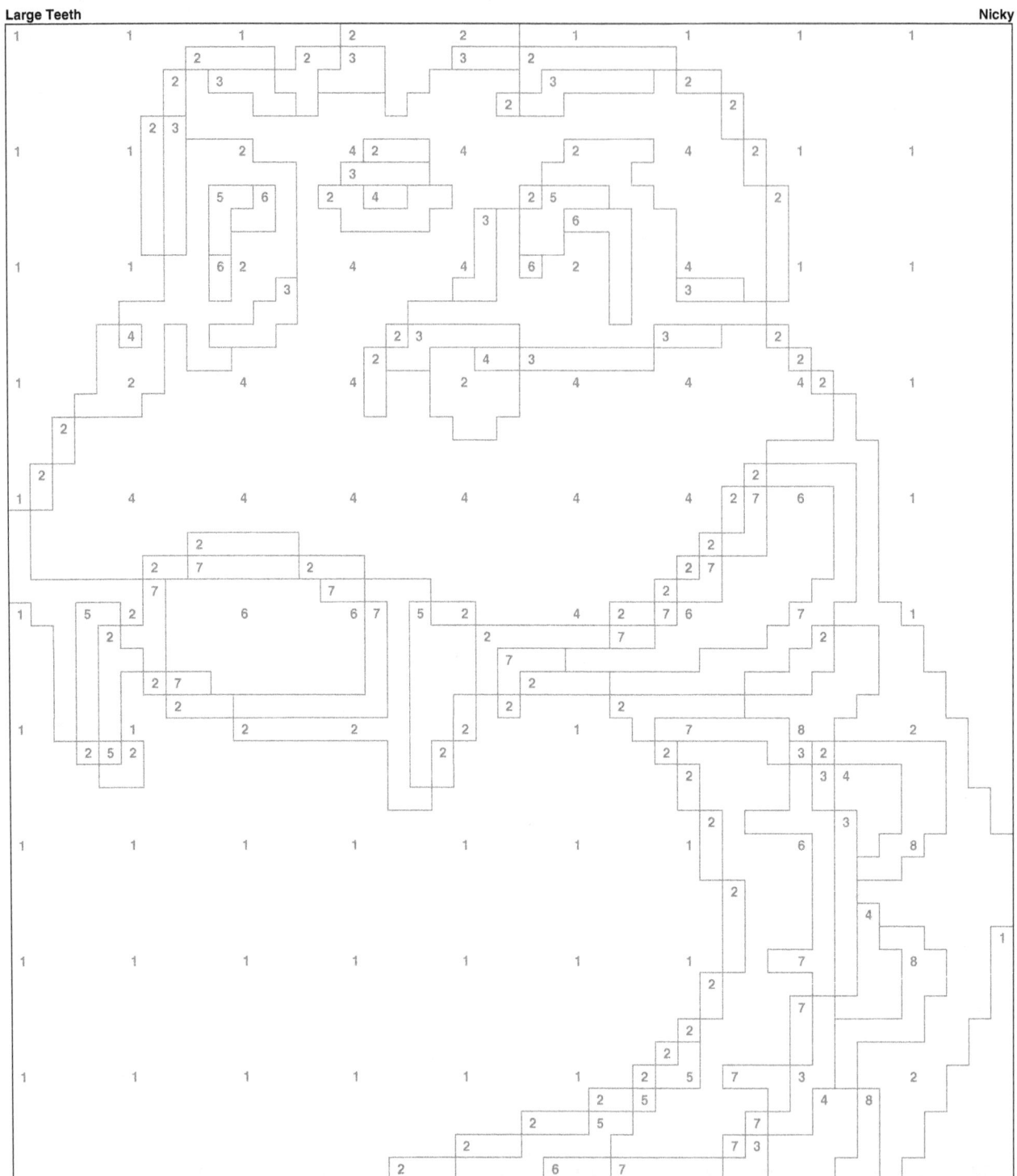

Daffy Duck — **Glucklich**

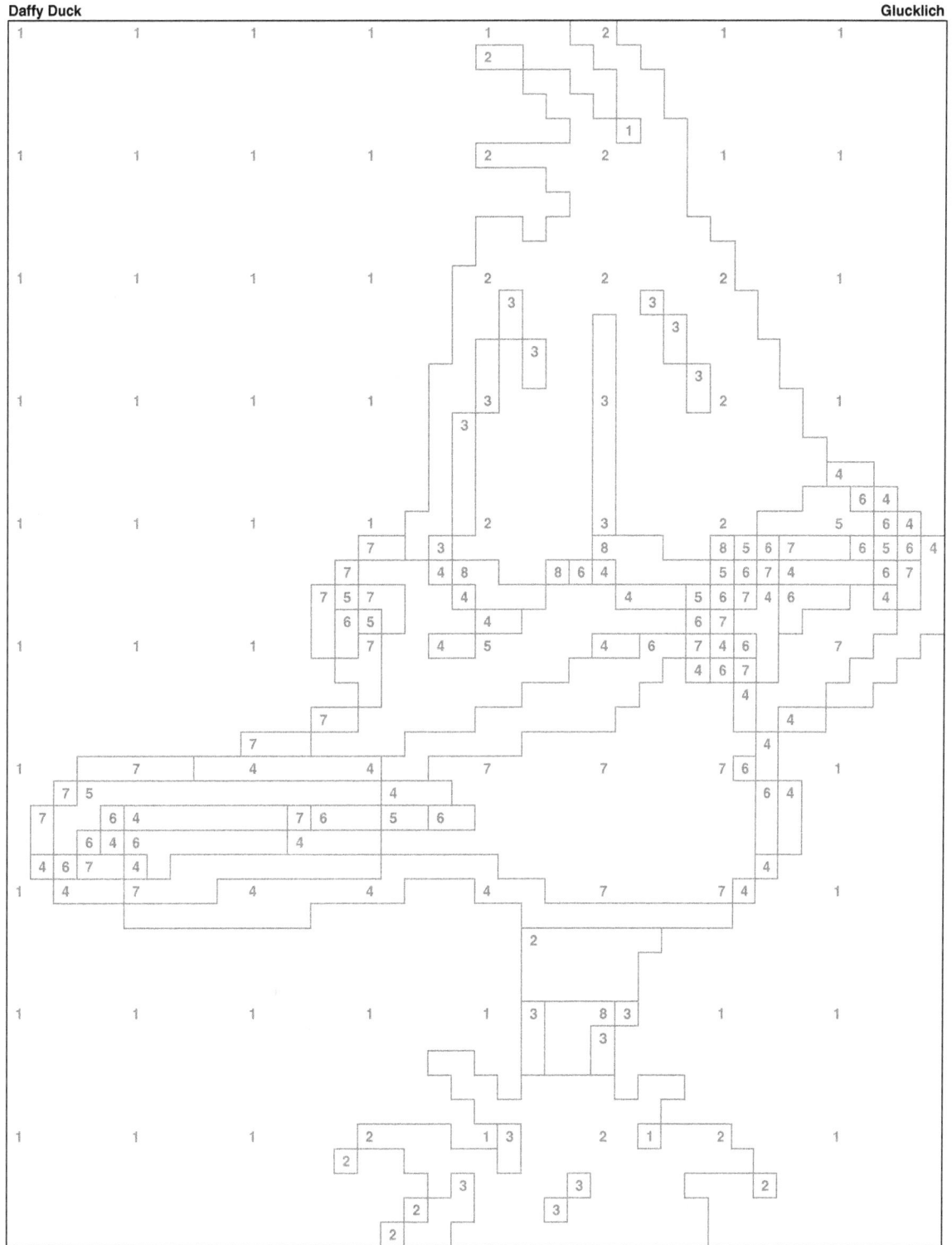

1-Macaroni and Cheese, 2-Black, 3-Manatee, 4-Fuzzy Wuzzy, 5-Burnt Orange, 6-Raw Sienna, 7-Brown, 8-White

Duplicate 0. Halloween Countdown: 20 Days to Go! wiggles

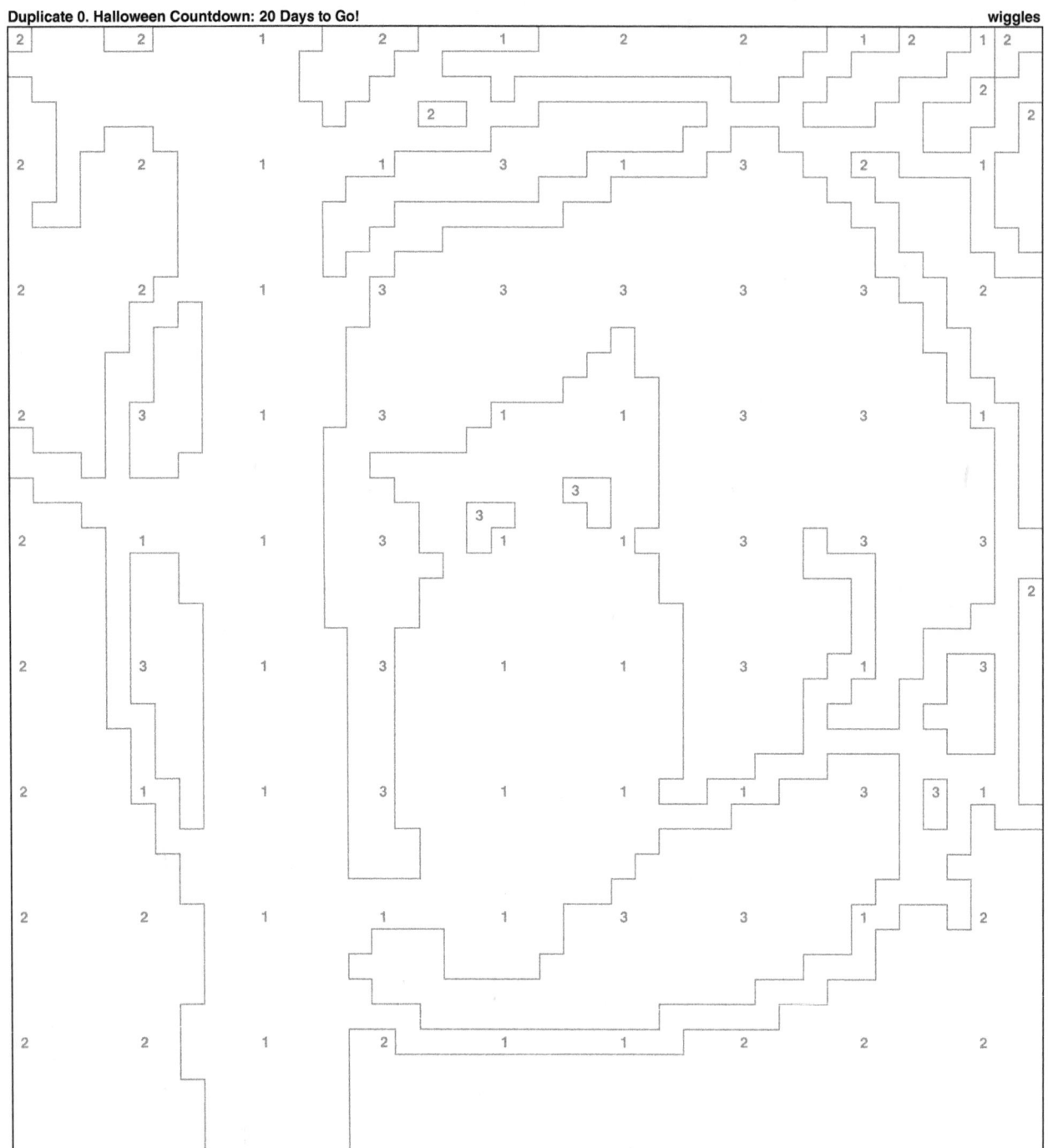

1-Black, 2-Midnight Blue, 3-Dandelion

1-Black, 2-Yellow-Orange, 3-Pig Pink, 4-Scarlet

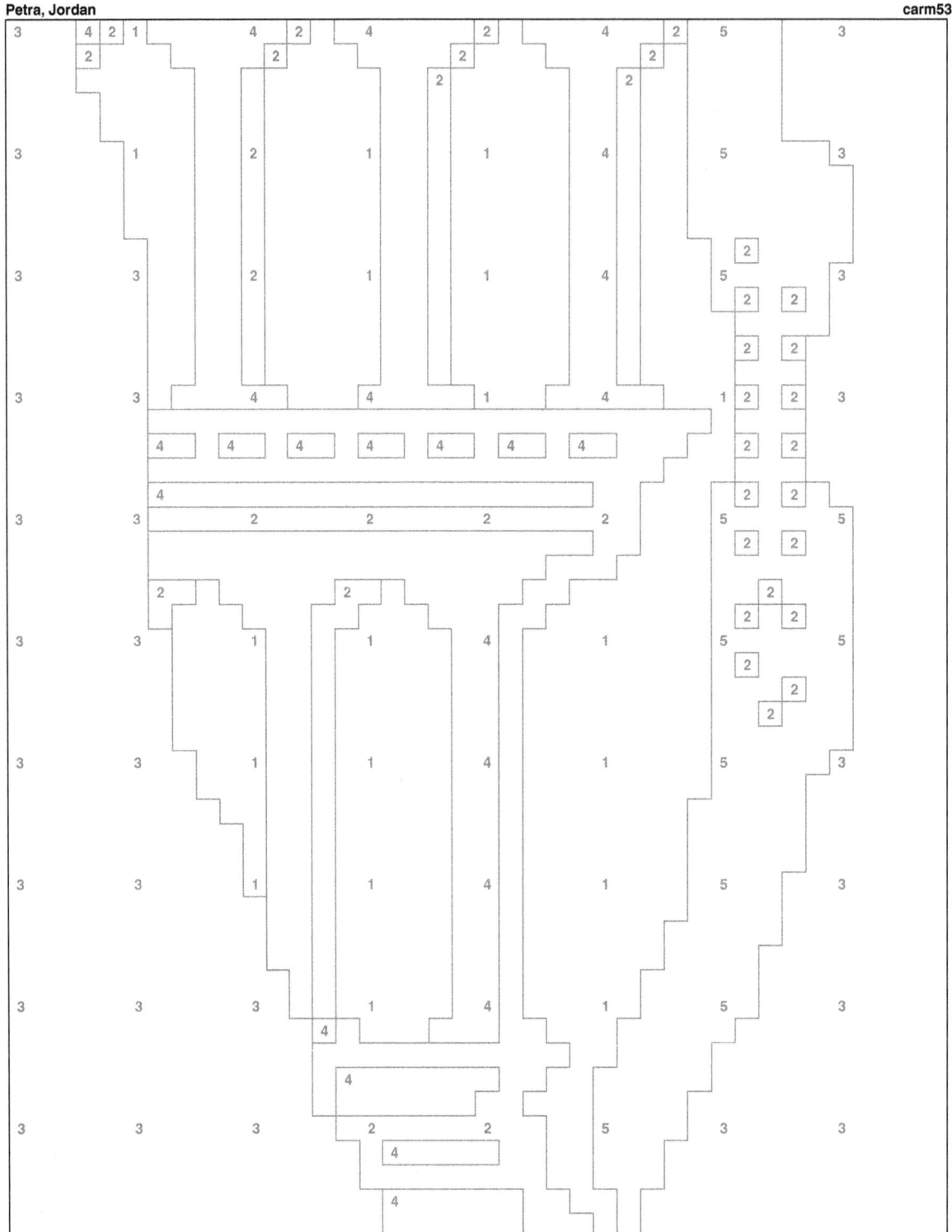

Mushroom

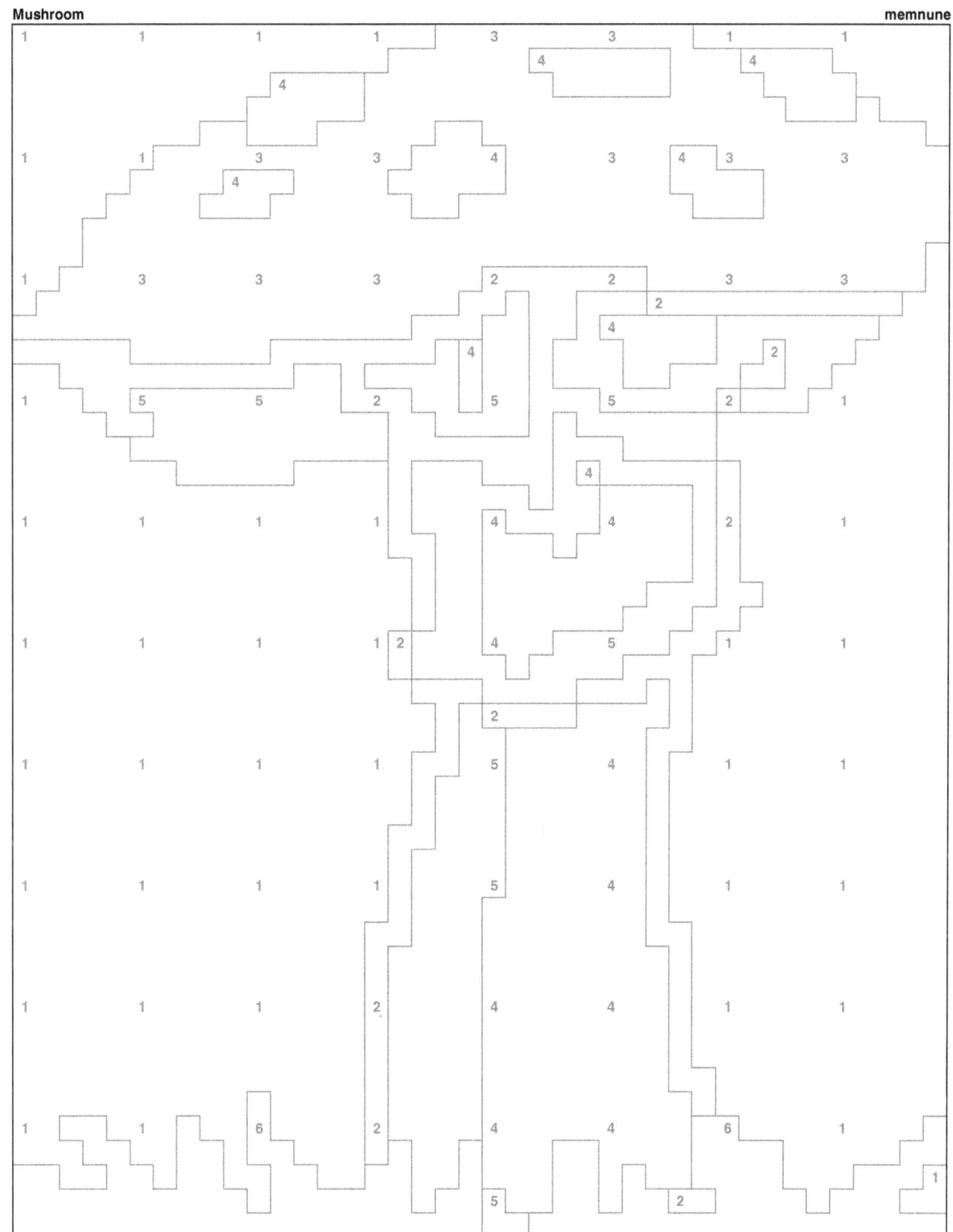

1-Timberwolf, 2-Tan, 3-Mahogany, 4-White, 5-Almond, 6-Tropical Rain Forest

Temple at Sundown   any_anthony

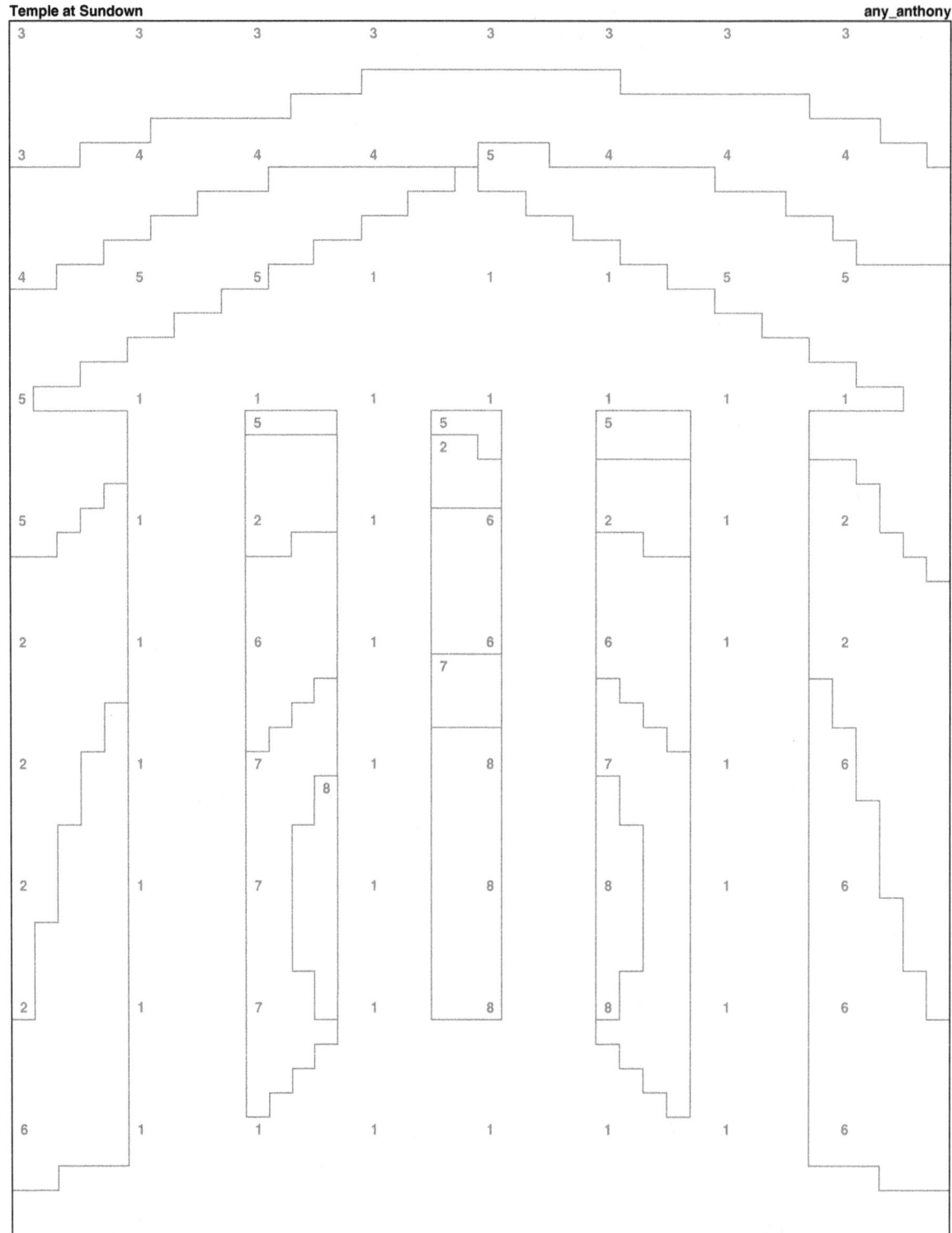

1-Black, 2-Scarlet, 3-Fuzzy Wuzzy, 4-Jazzberry Jam, 5-Mahogany, 6-Red-Orange, 7-Mango Tango, 8-Dandelion

Odd Little Creature — lilyania

1-Denim, 2-Cerulean, 3-Indigo, 4-Black, 5-Cerise, 6-Jazzberry Jam, 7-Cadet Blue

Drink Me popkin

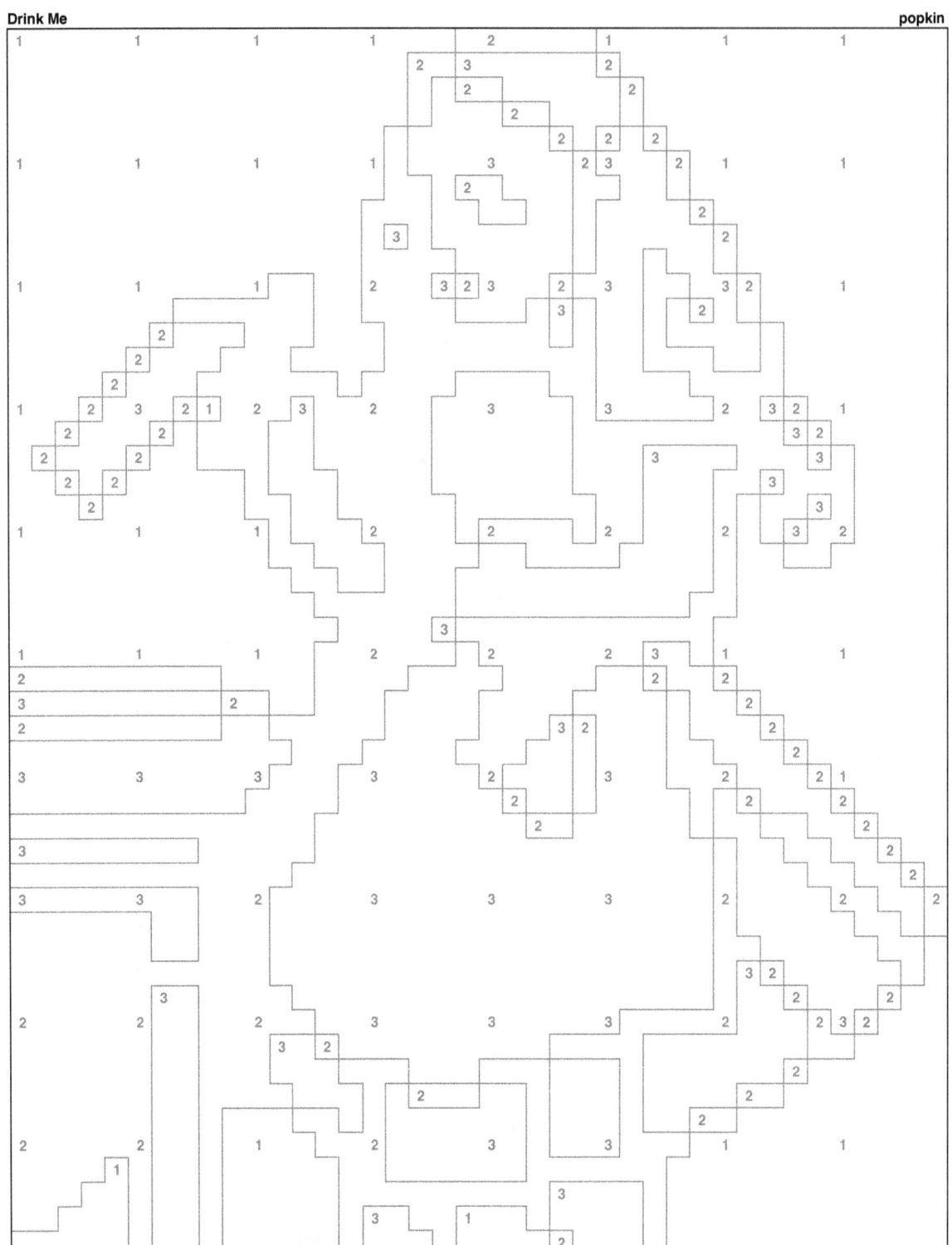

1-Cornflower, 2-Black, 3-White

Seahorse — Eilleen

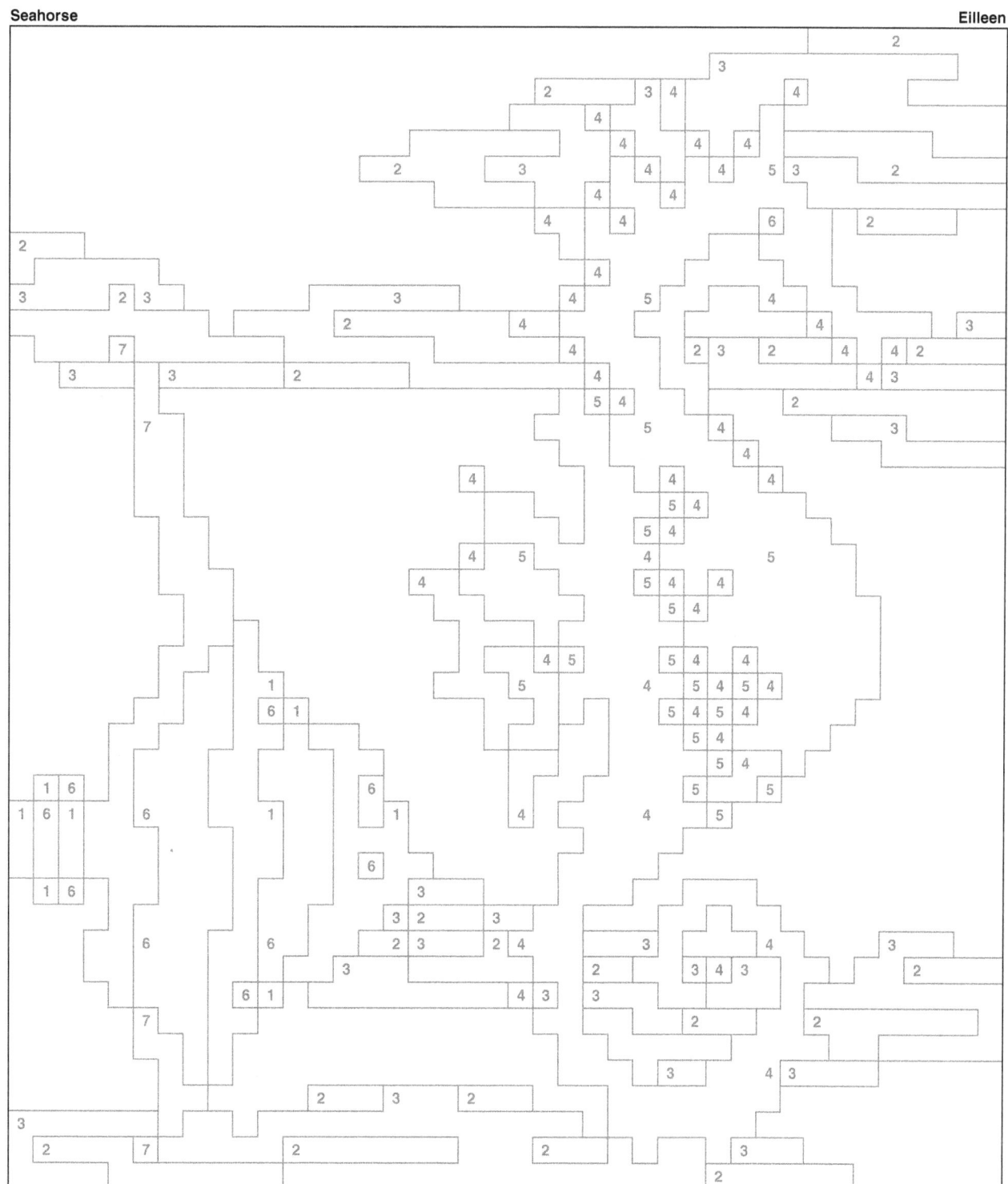

1-Yellow-Orange, 2-Blue (III), 3-Robin's Egg Blue, 4-Tropical Rain Forest, 5-Caribbean Green, 6-Black, 7-Red-Orange

Grapes

1-Scarlet, 2-Tropical Rain Forest, 3-Black, 4-Jazzberry Jam

Kitty Reading

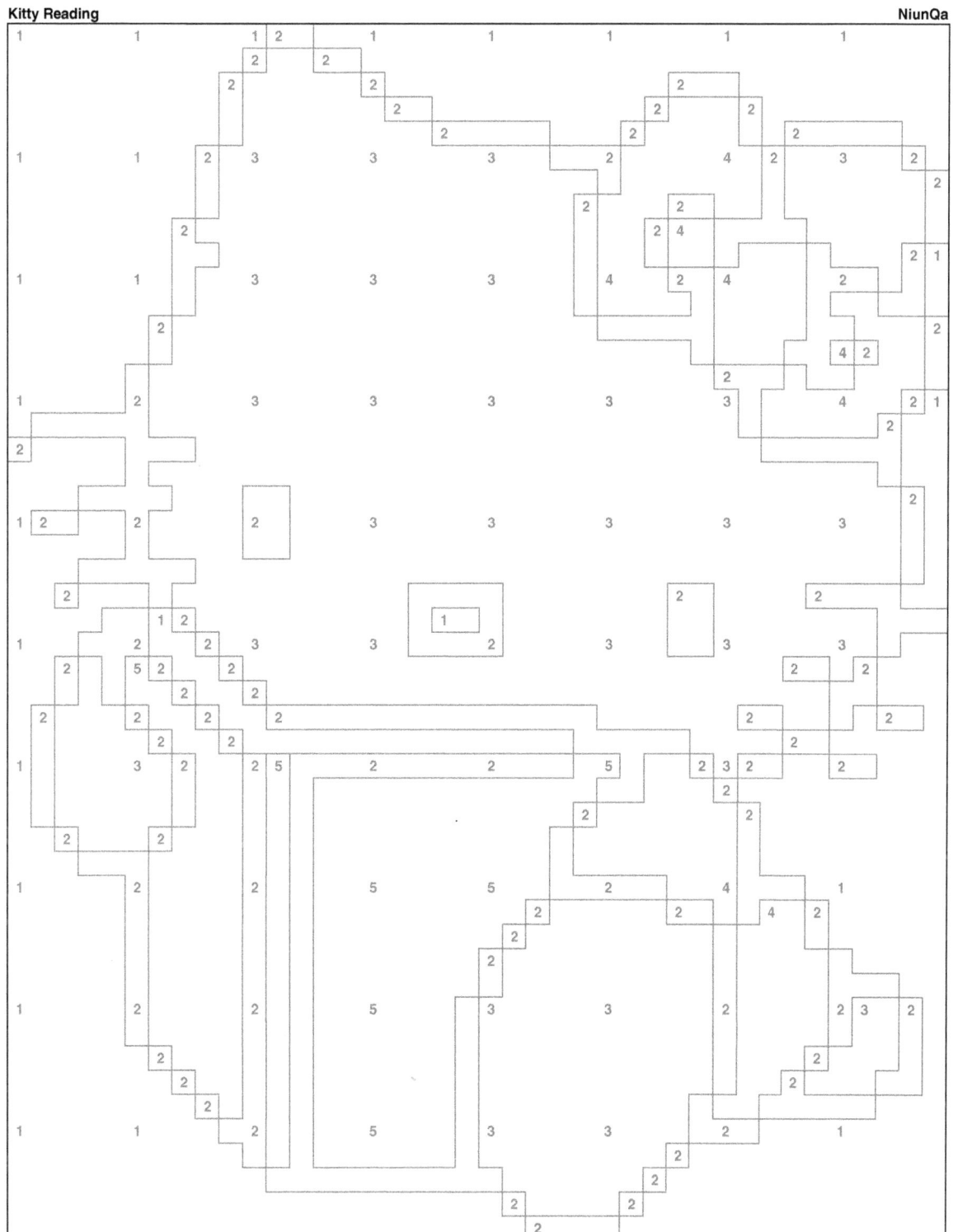

1-Canary, 2-Black, 3-White, 4-Pig Pink, 5-Periwinkle

Minnie Mouse

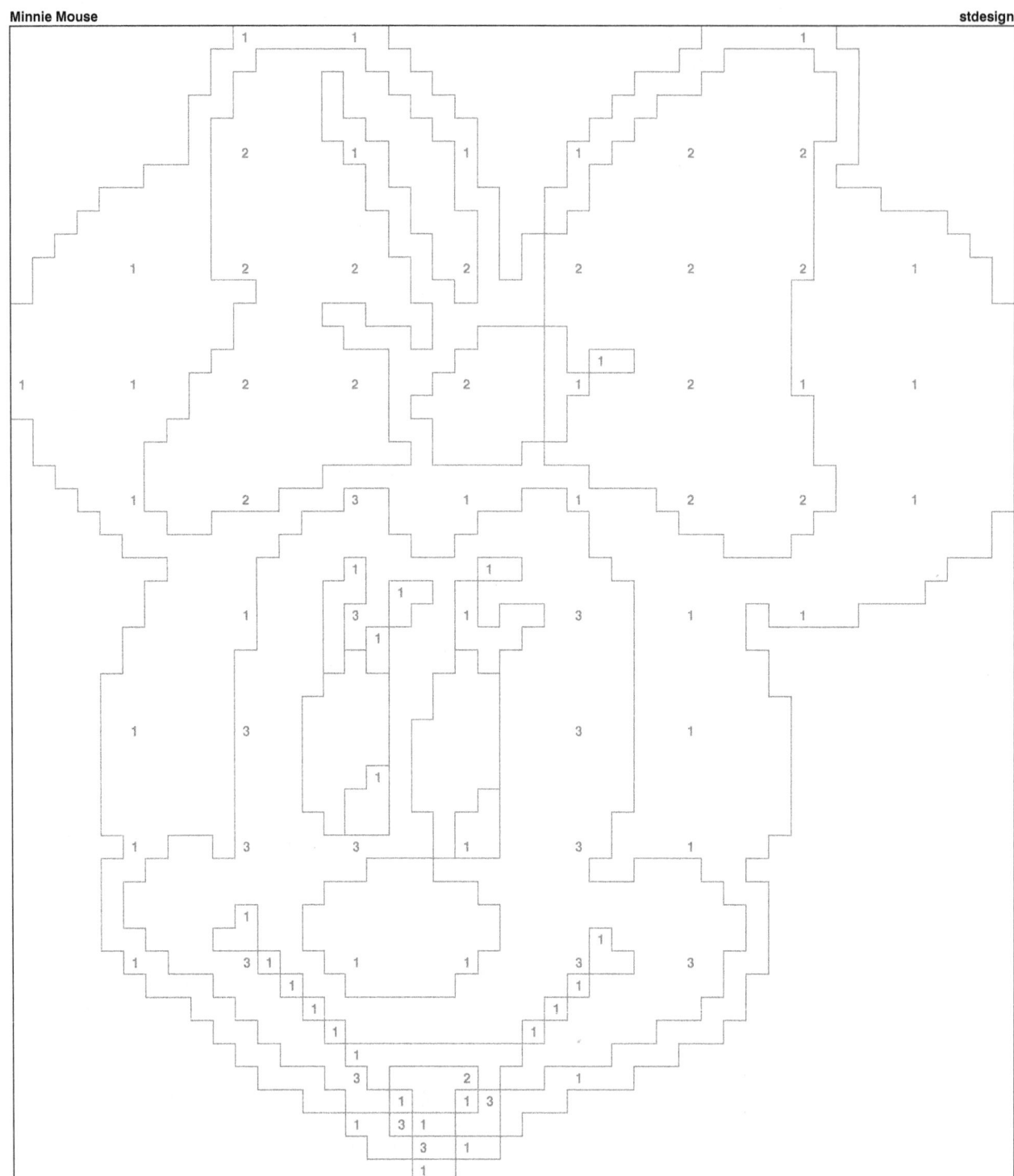

1-Black, 2-Bittersweet, 3-Peach

Santa Claus

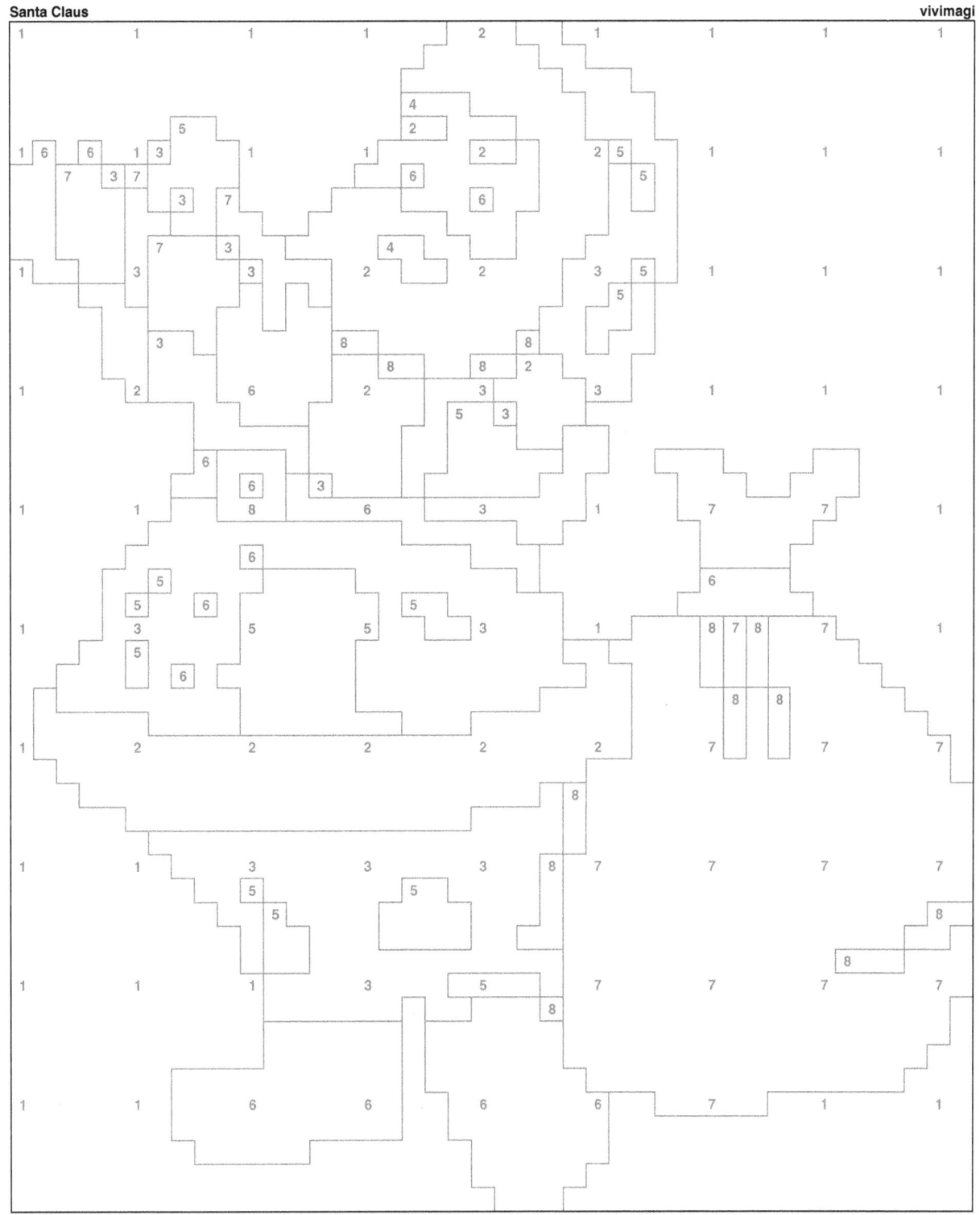

1-Midnight Blue, 2-White, 3-Maroon, 4-Tumbleweed, 5-Sunset Orange, 6-Outer Space, 7-Tropical Rain Forest, 8-Shadow

Teddy Nicky

1-Black, 2-Raw Sienna, 3-Tumbleweed, 4-Pig Pink

Wolf Silhouette DrDoris

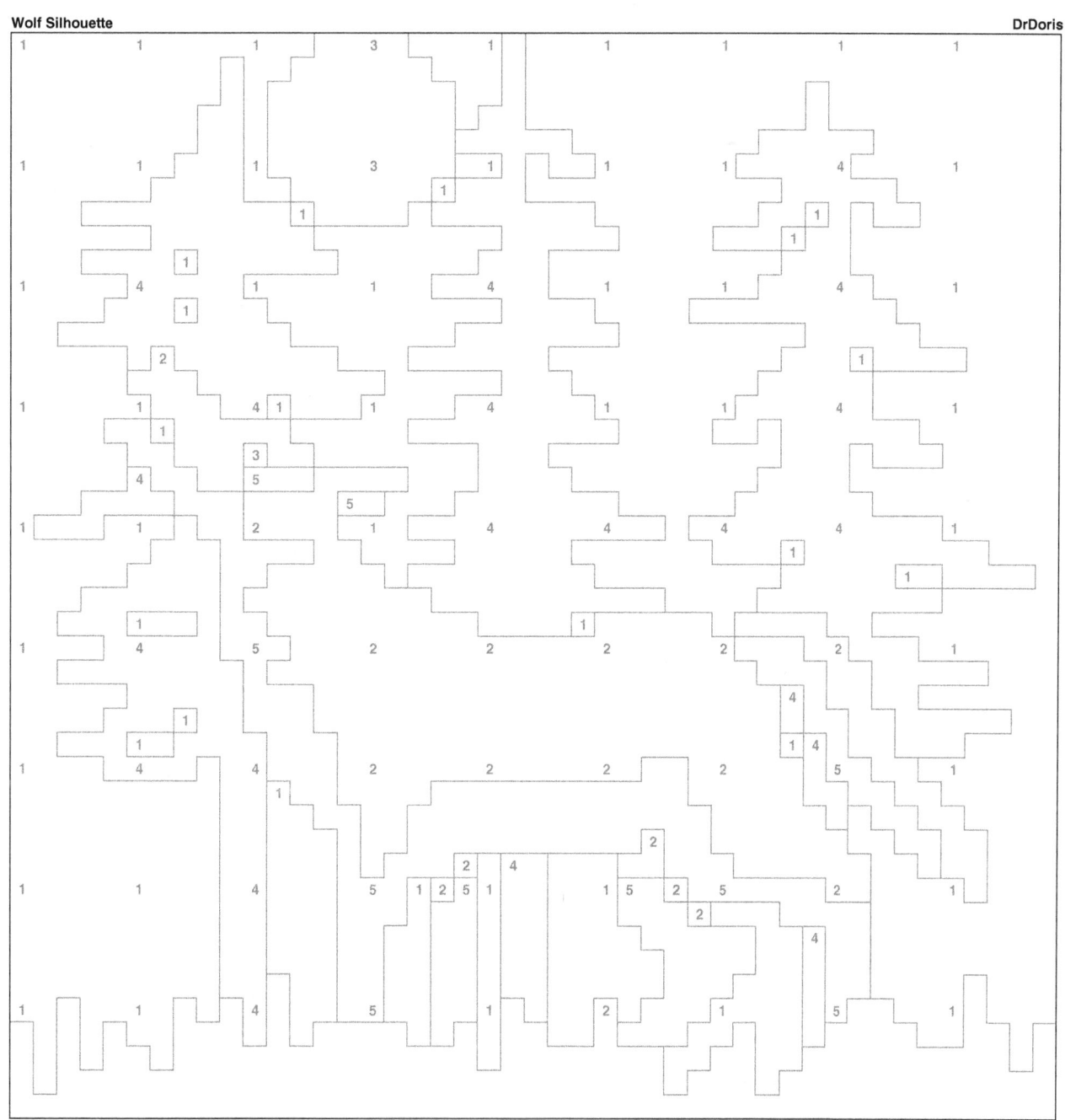

1-Raw Sienna, 2-Fuzzy Wuzzy, 3-Almond, 4-Tumbleweed, 5-Outer Space

Jack Russel Puppy skybreezes

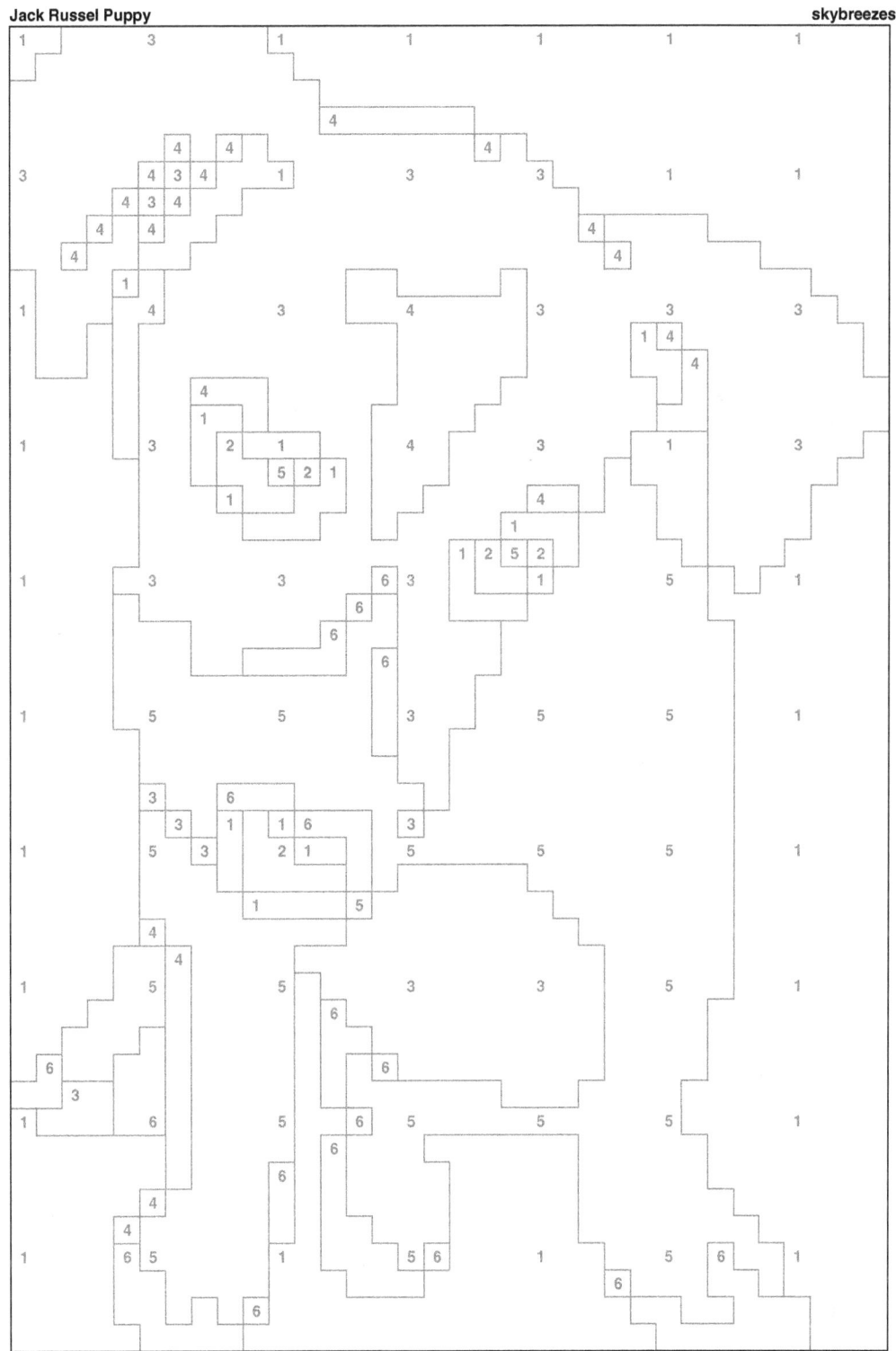

1-Fuzzy Wuzzy, 2-Black, 3-Mango Tango, 4-Goldenrod, 5-White, 6-Manatee

Tired Cat beren2005

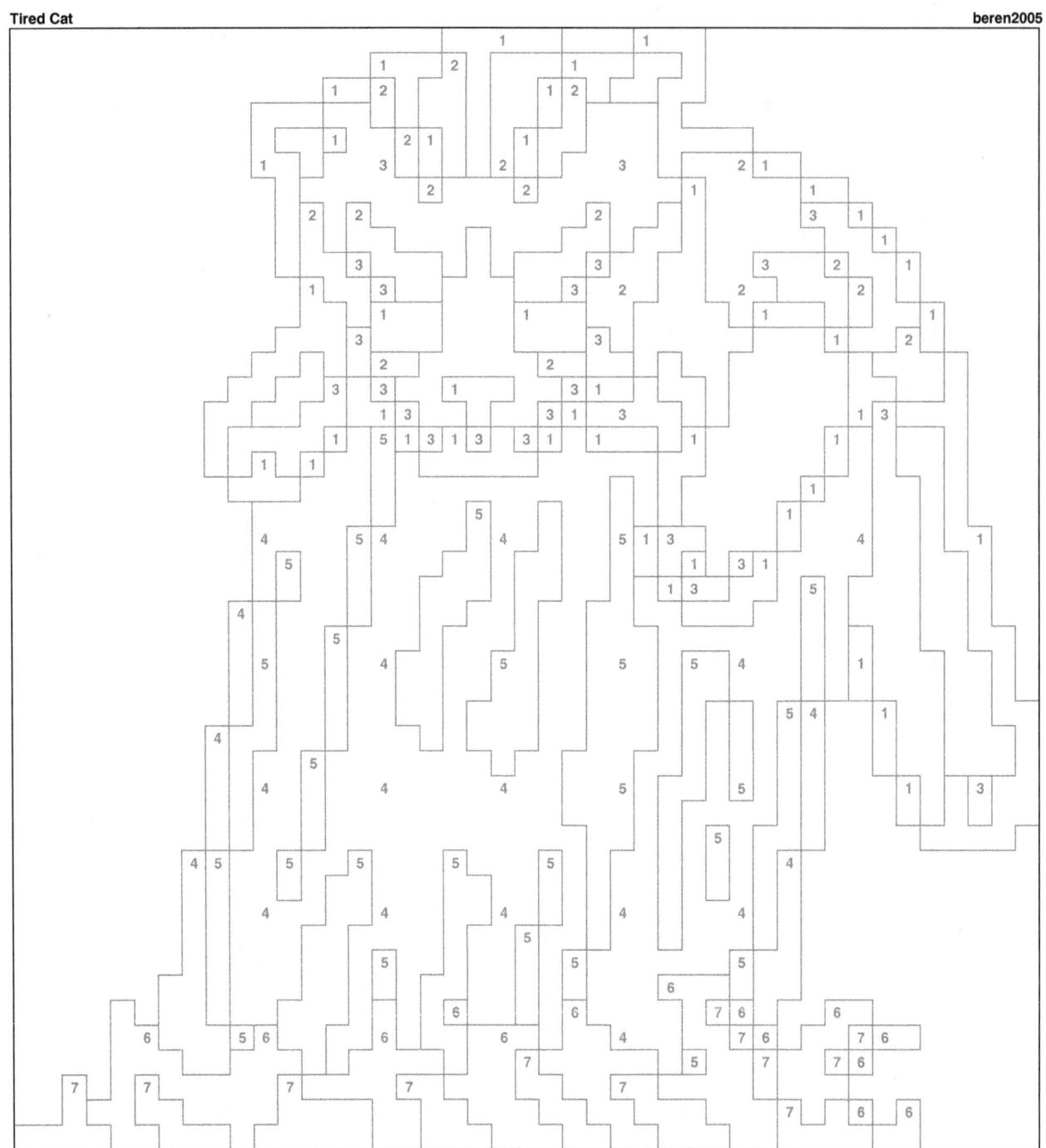

1-Black, 2-Beaver, 3-Yellow-Orange, 4-Fuzzy Wuzzy, 5-Raw Sienna, 6-Green, 7-Asparagus

Snake Minoo

1-Black, 2-Fuzzy Wuzzy, 3-Yellow-Orange, 4-Cadet Blue, 5-Sunset Orange

Final Fantasy III - Troll Maedhros

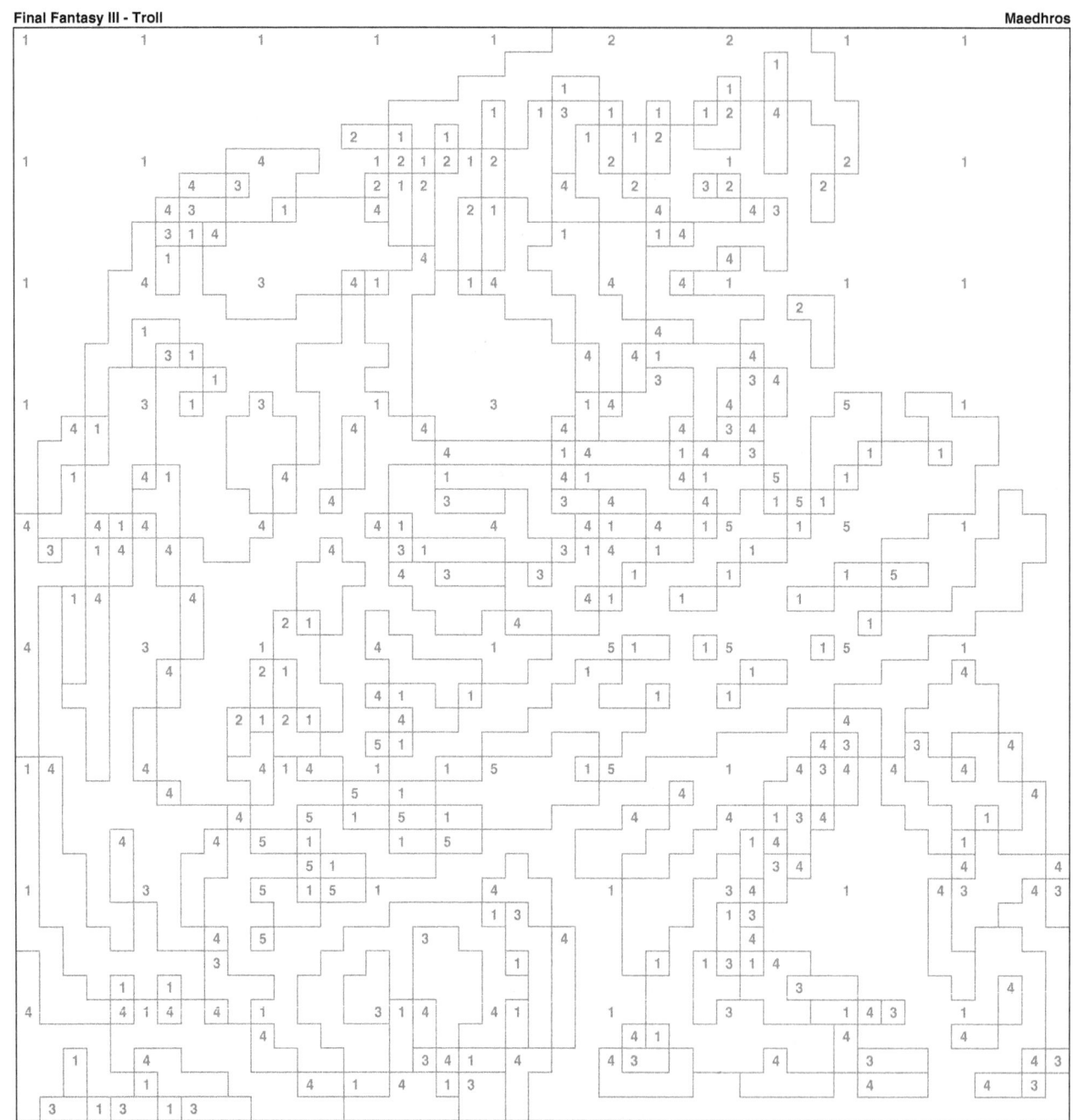

1-Black, 2-Tropical Rain Forest, 3-Timberwolf, 4-Asparagus, 5-Red-Orange

Puppy zjmonty

1-Timberwolf, 2-Outer Space, 3-White, 4-Tumbleweed, 5-Eggplant, 6-Tan

Asian Tapir — Glucklich

1-Beaver, 2-Black, 3-Manatee, 4-Shadow, 5-Eggplant

Tiger — Nicky

1-Mango Tango, 2-Fuzzy Wuzzy, 3-Burnt Orange, 4-Green-Yellow, 5-Outer Space, 6-Dandelion, 7-White, 8-Maroon

Terminator mudshark

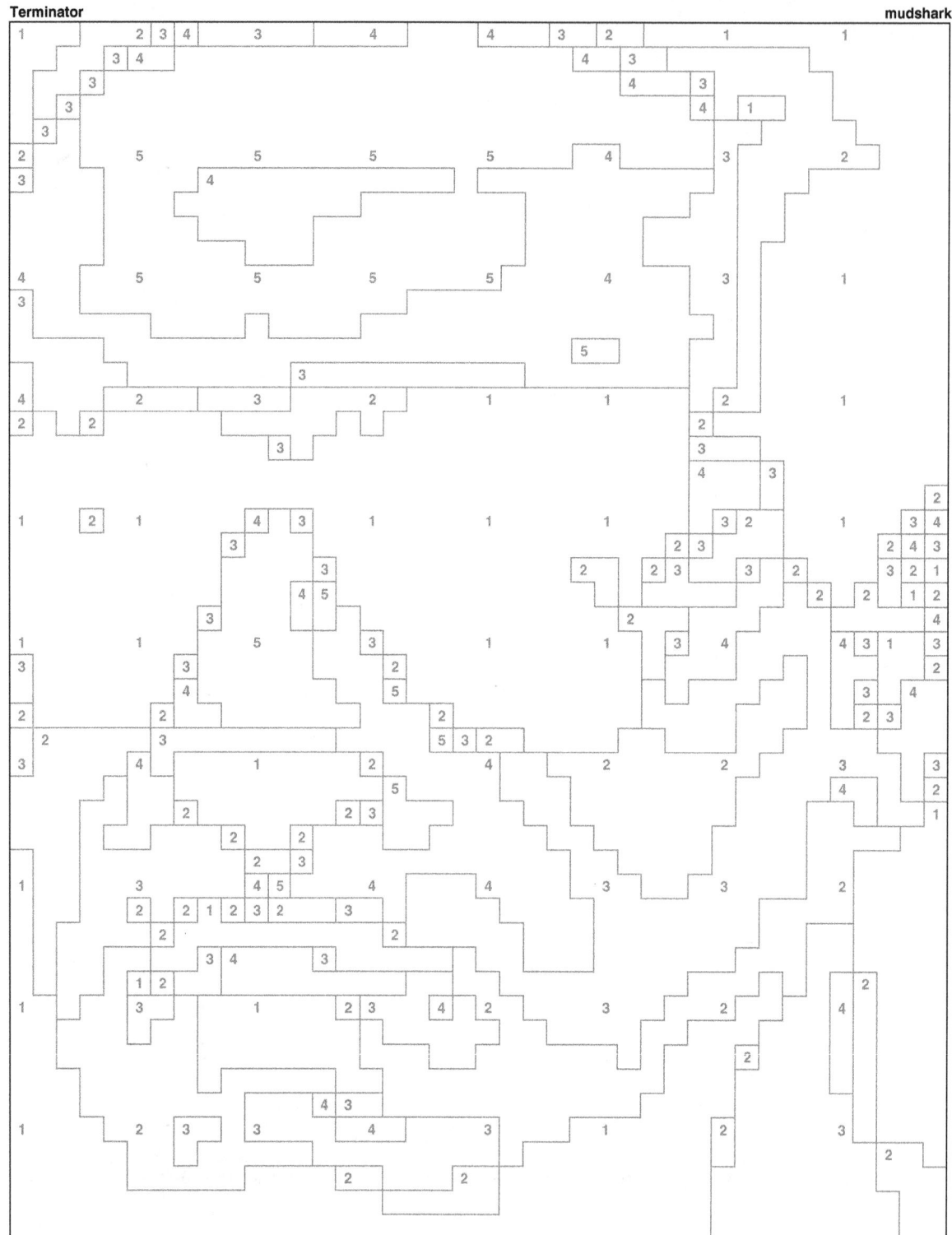

1-Black, 2-Outer Space, 3-Manatee, 4-Cadet Blue, 5-White

1-Black, 2-Granny Smith Apple, 3-Red-Orange, 4-Maroon, 5-Mango Tango, 6-Dandelion

Common Kingfisher   **Glucklich**

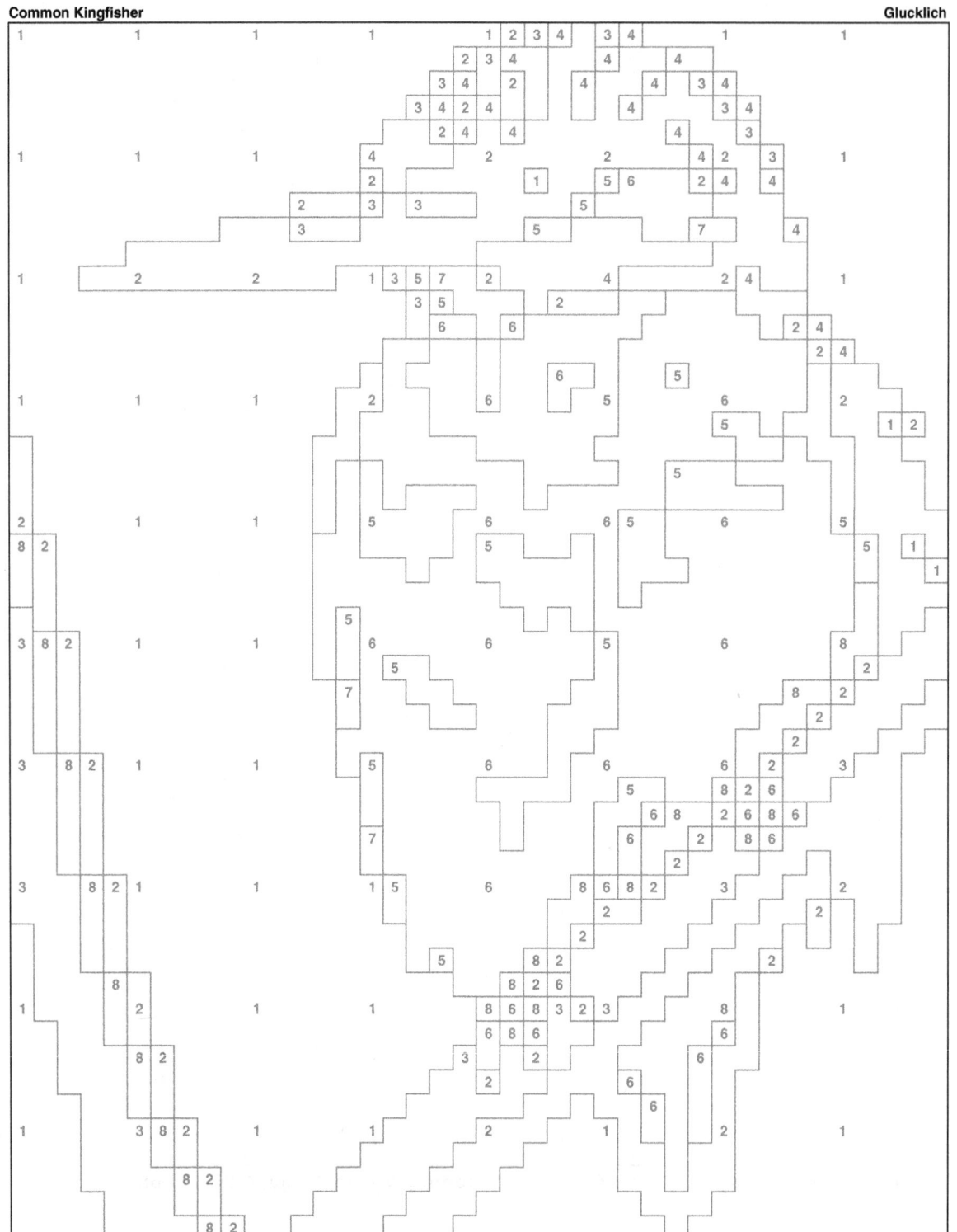

1-Tumbleweed, 2-Black, 3-Eggplant, 4-Blue-Green, 5-Raw Sienna, 6-Indian Red, 7-White, 8-Fuzzy Wuzzy

Mushrooms

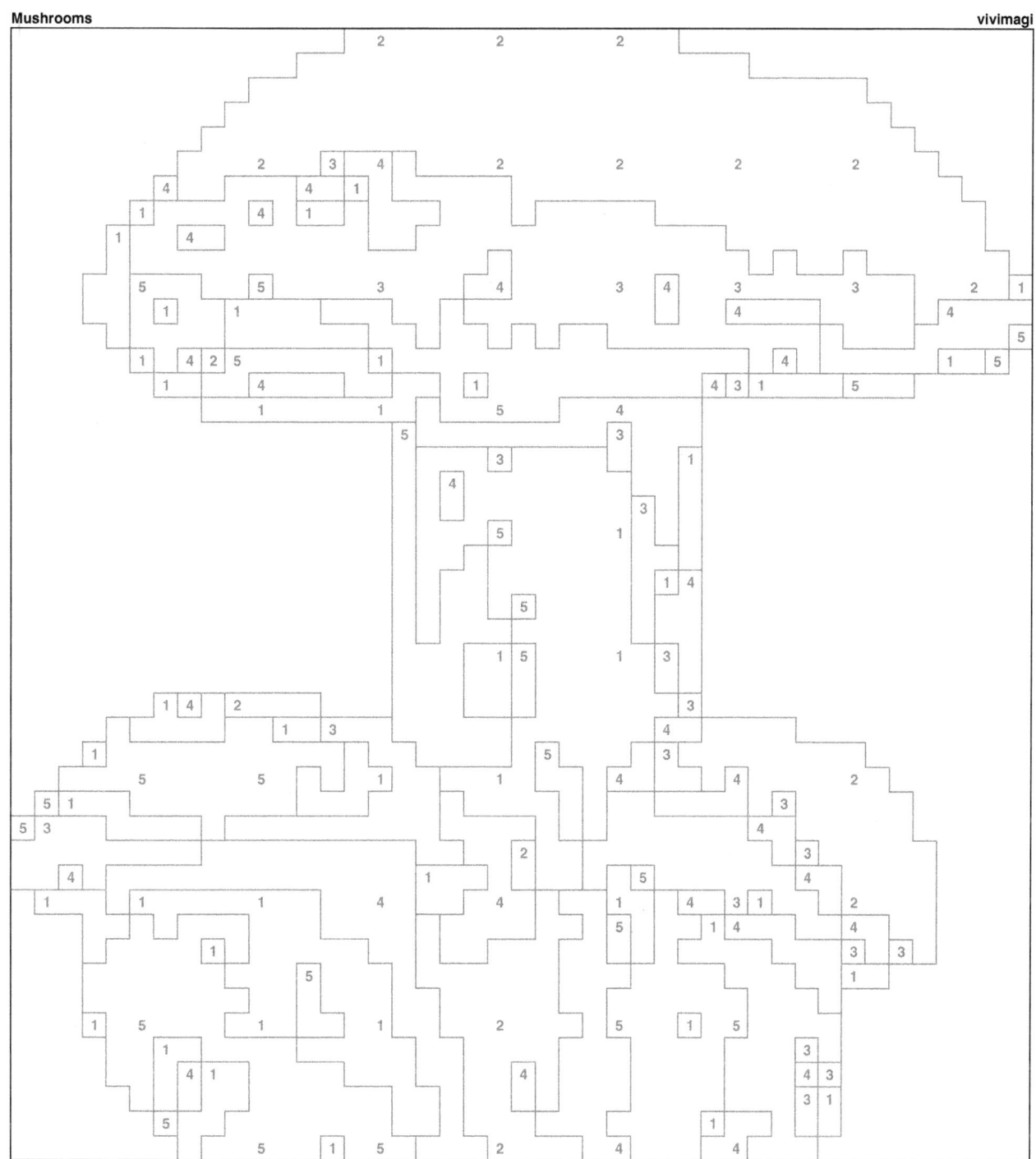

1-Tan, 2-Eggplant, 3-Raw Sienna, 4-Beaver, 5-Peach

Self Portrait

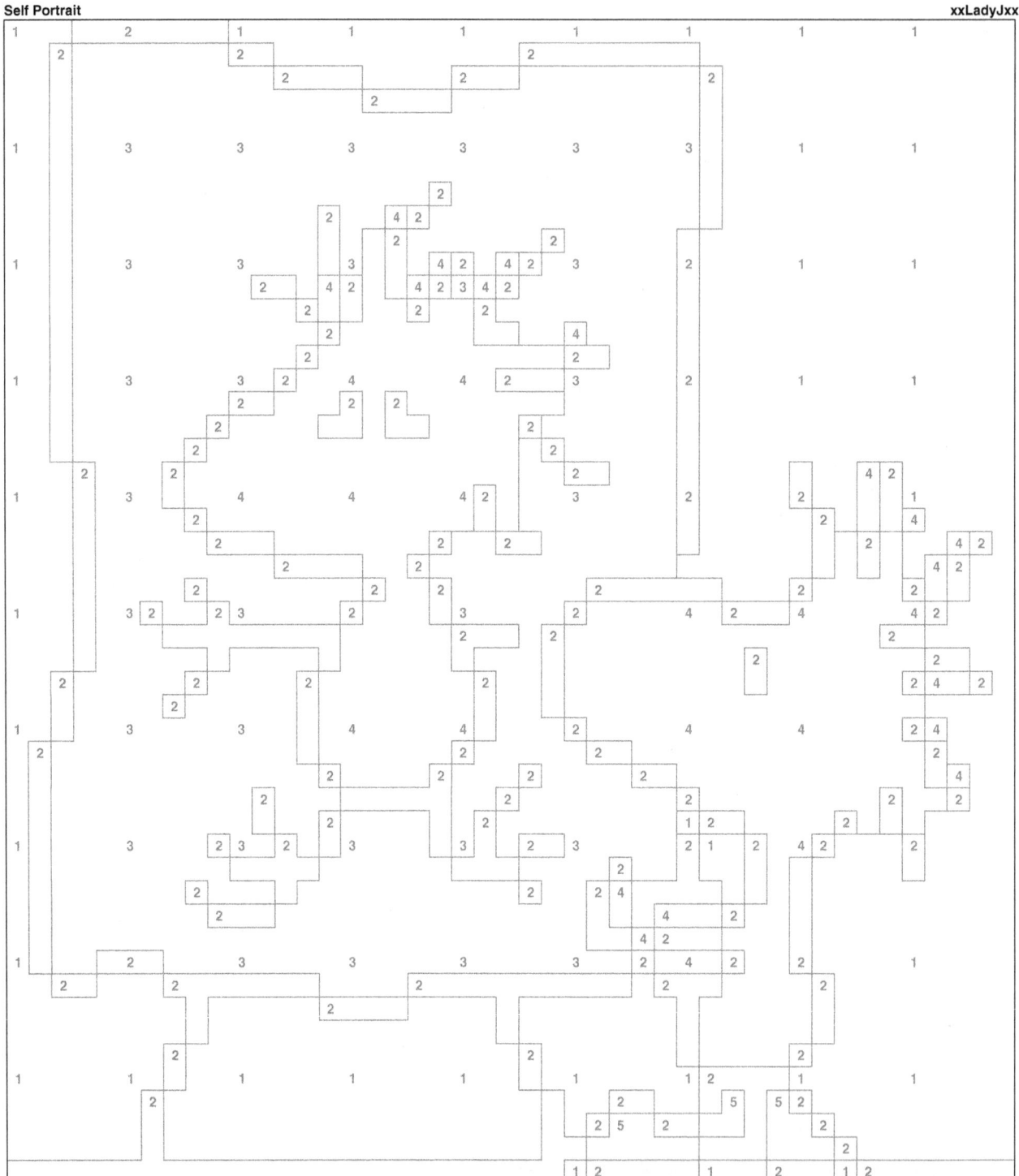

1-Aquamarine, 2-Black, 3-Banana Mania, 4-Yellow, 5-Yellow-Orange

The Nightmare Before Christmas - Sally

1-Periwinkle, 2-Black, 3-Manatee, 4-Shadow, 5-Pig Pink, 6-Fuzzy Wuzzy

Girl with a Pearl Earring — popkin

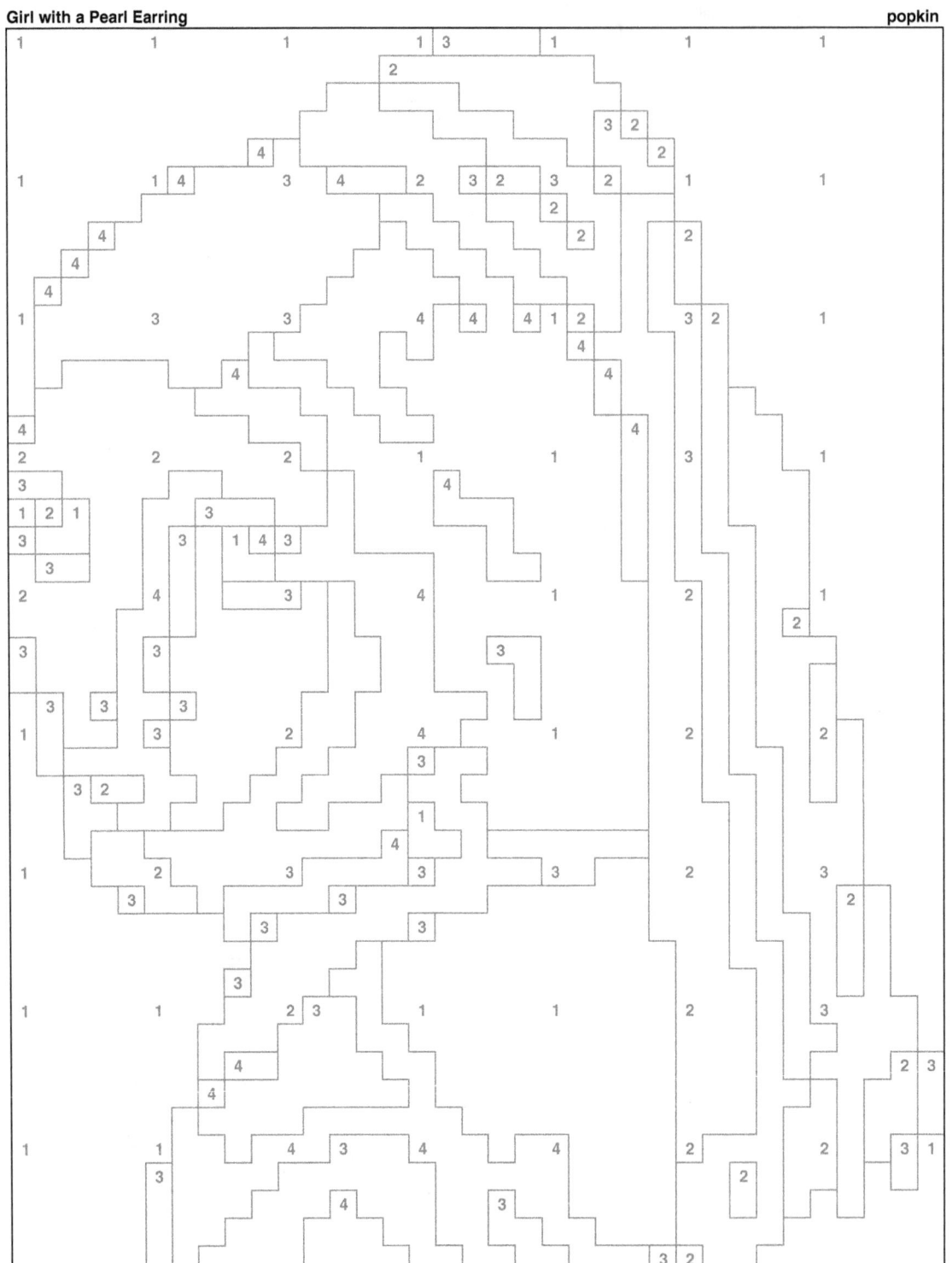

1-Black, 2-White, 3-Timberwolf, 4-Manatee

Boat at Sunset — Nicky

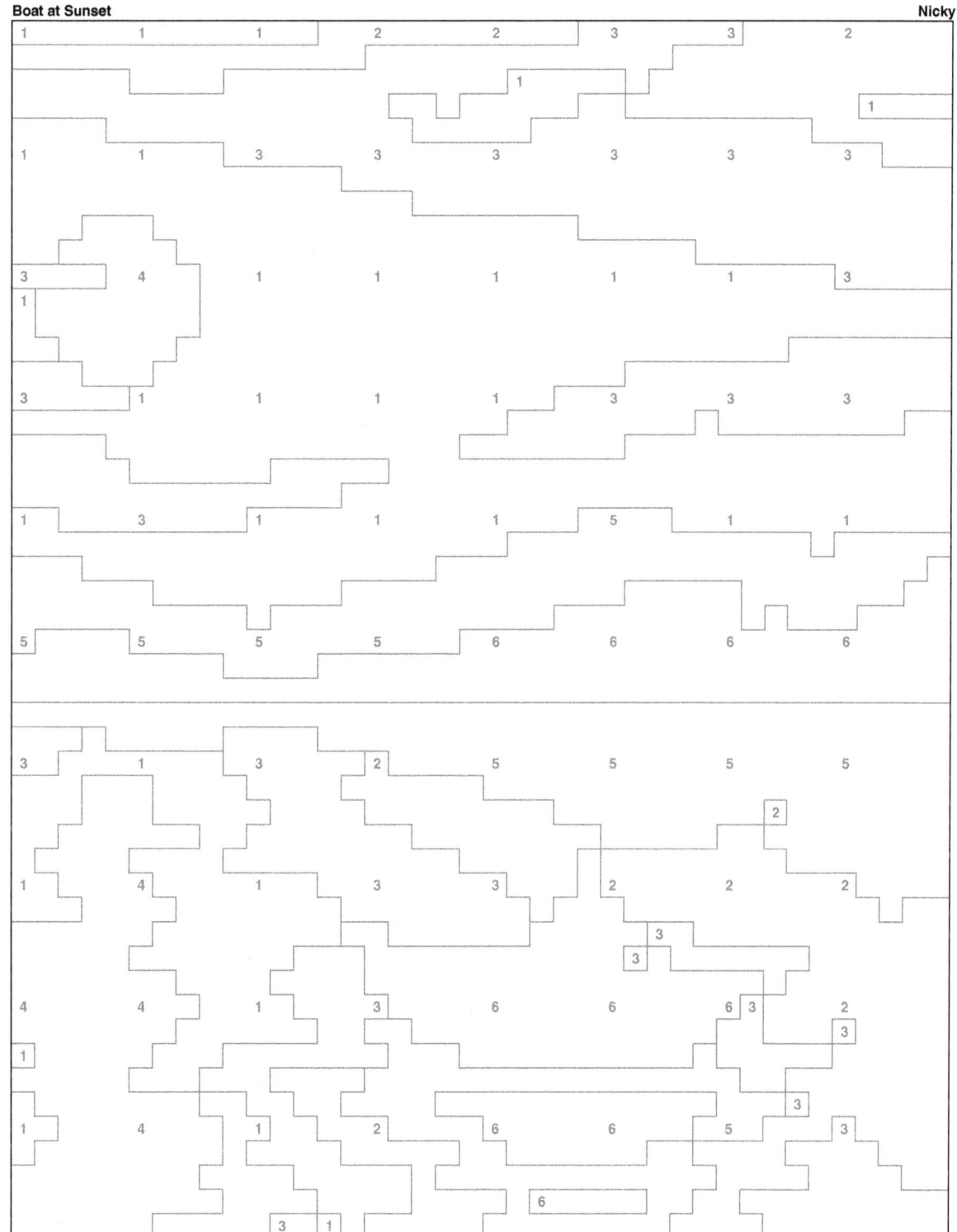

1-Goldenrod, 2-Burnt Sienna, 3-Yellow-Orange, 4-White, 5-Mahogany, 6-Black

Who Left the Light On?

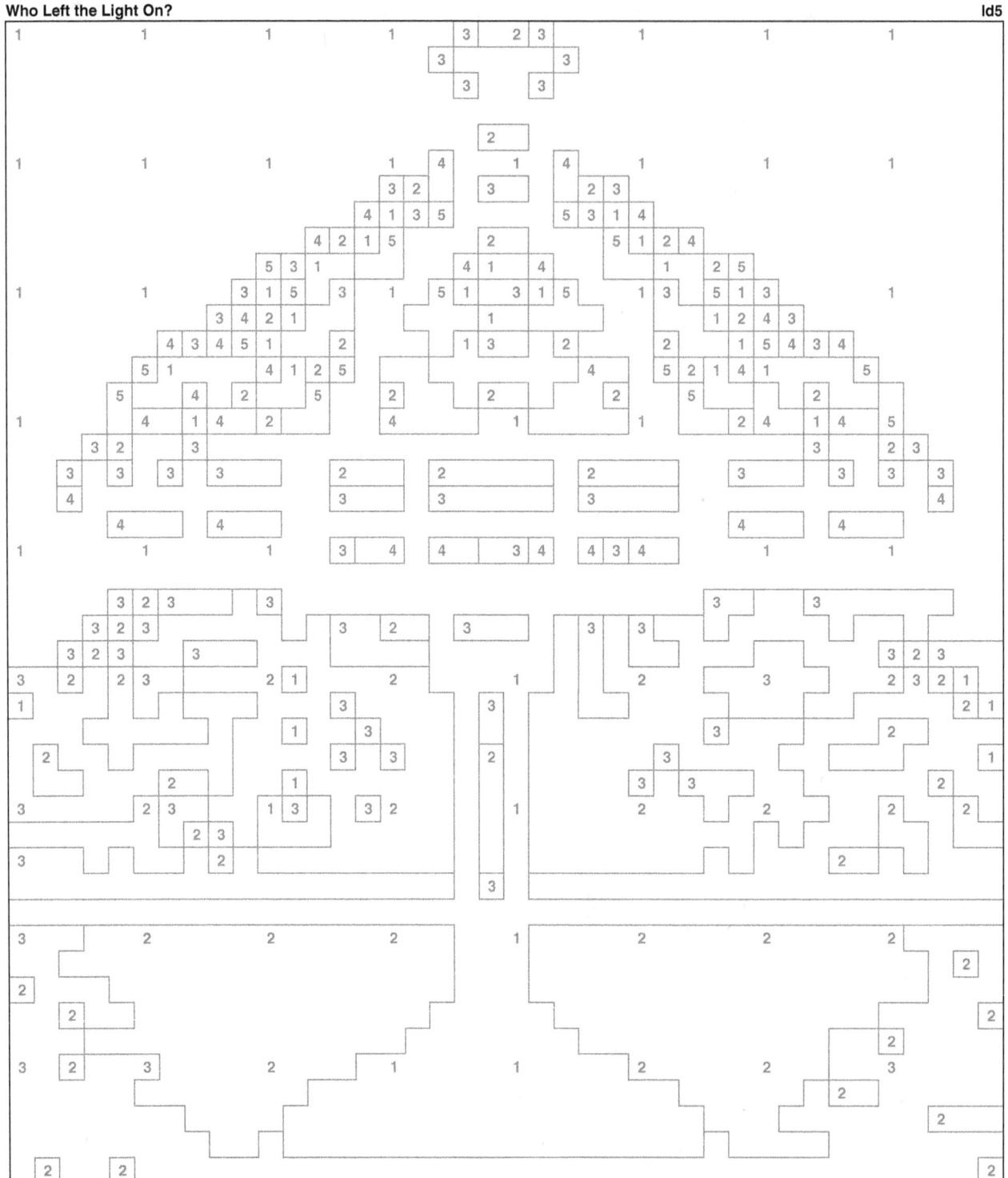

1-Black, 2-White, 3-Yellow-Orange, 4-Inchworm, 5-Burnt Orange

Raspberries — memnune

1-Outer Space, 2-Inchworm, 3-Yellow-Green, 4-Scarlet, 5-Bittersweet

Duplicate 0. Donald Duck talanimal

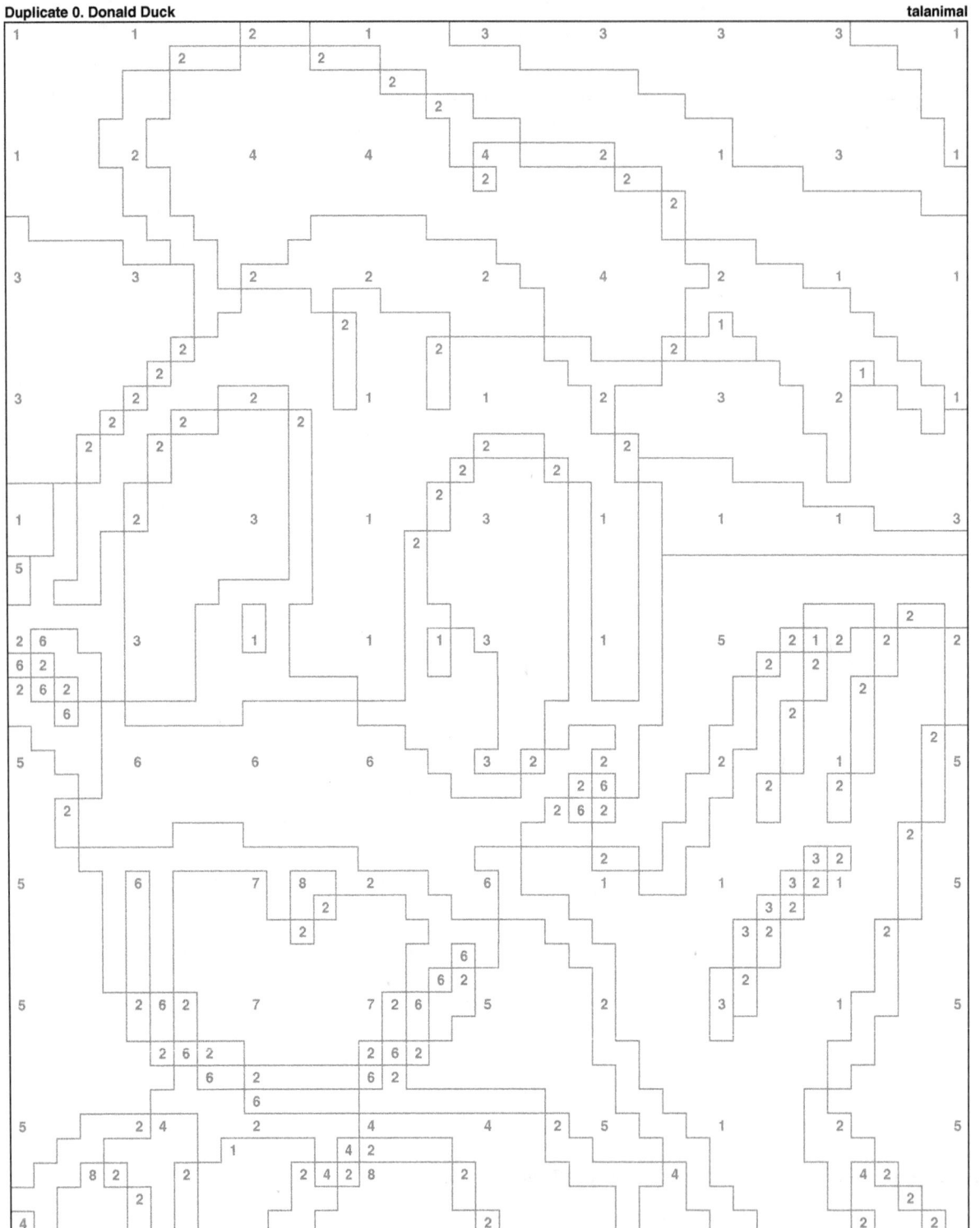

1-White, 2-Black, 3-Periwinkle, 4-Wild Blue Yonder, 5-Olive Green, 6-Yellow-Orange, 7-Orange, 8-Burnt Sienna

Hippo griddlock

1-Timberwolf, 2-Black, 3-Manatee, 4-White

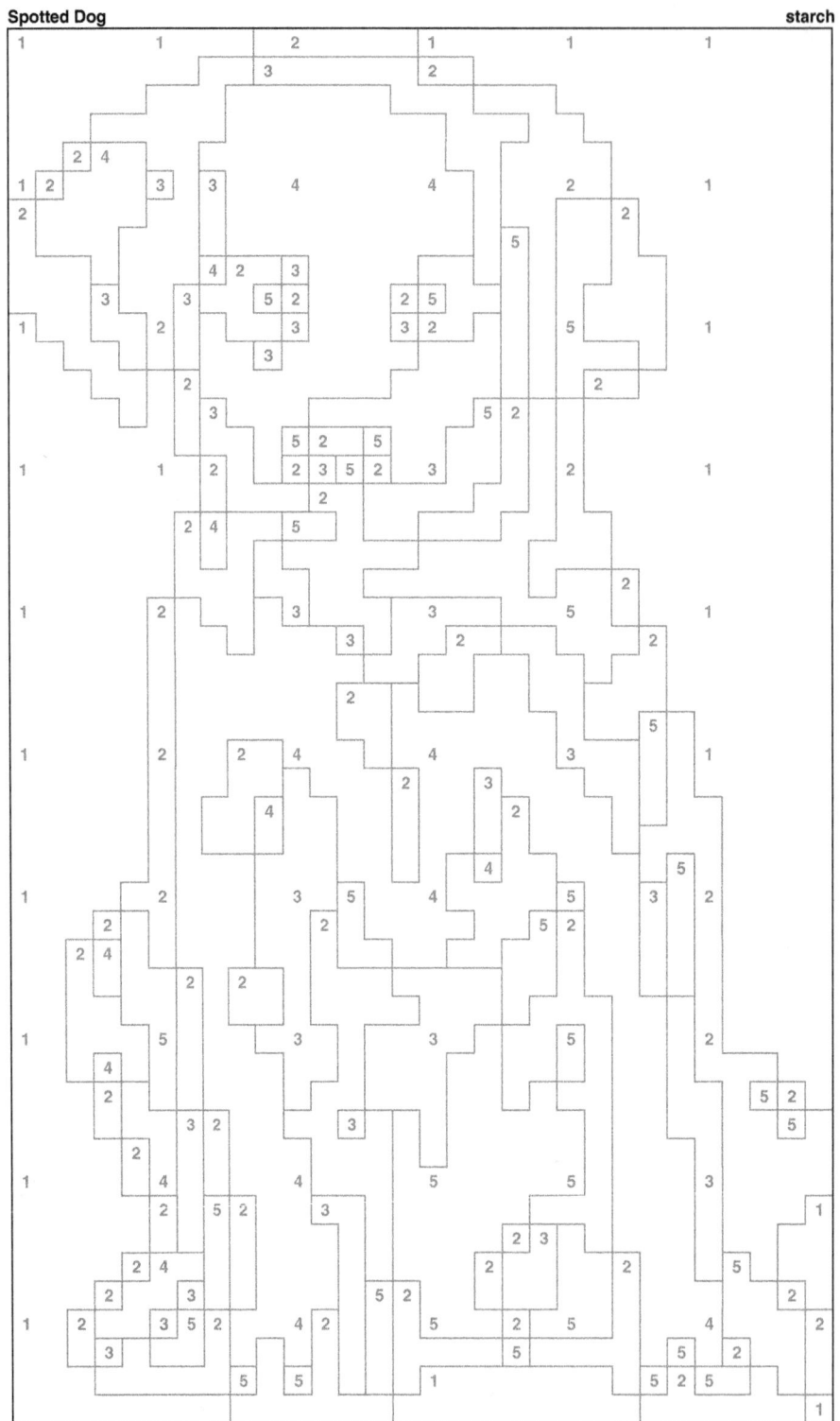

1-Green, 2-Black, 3-Cadet Blue, 4-White, 5-Manatee

Santa Claus willem

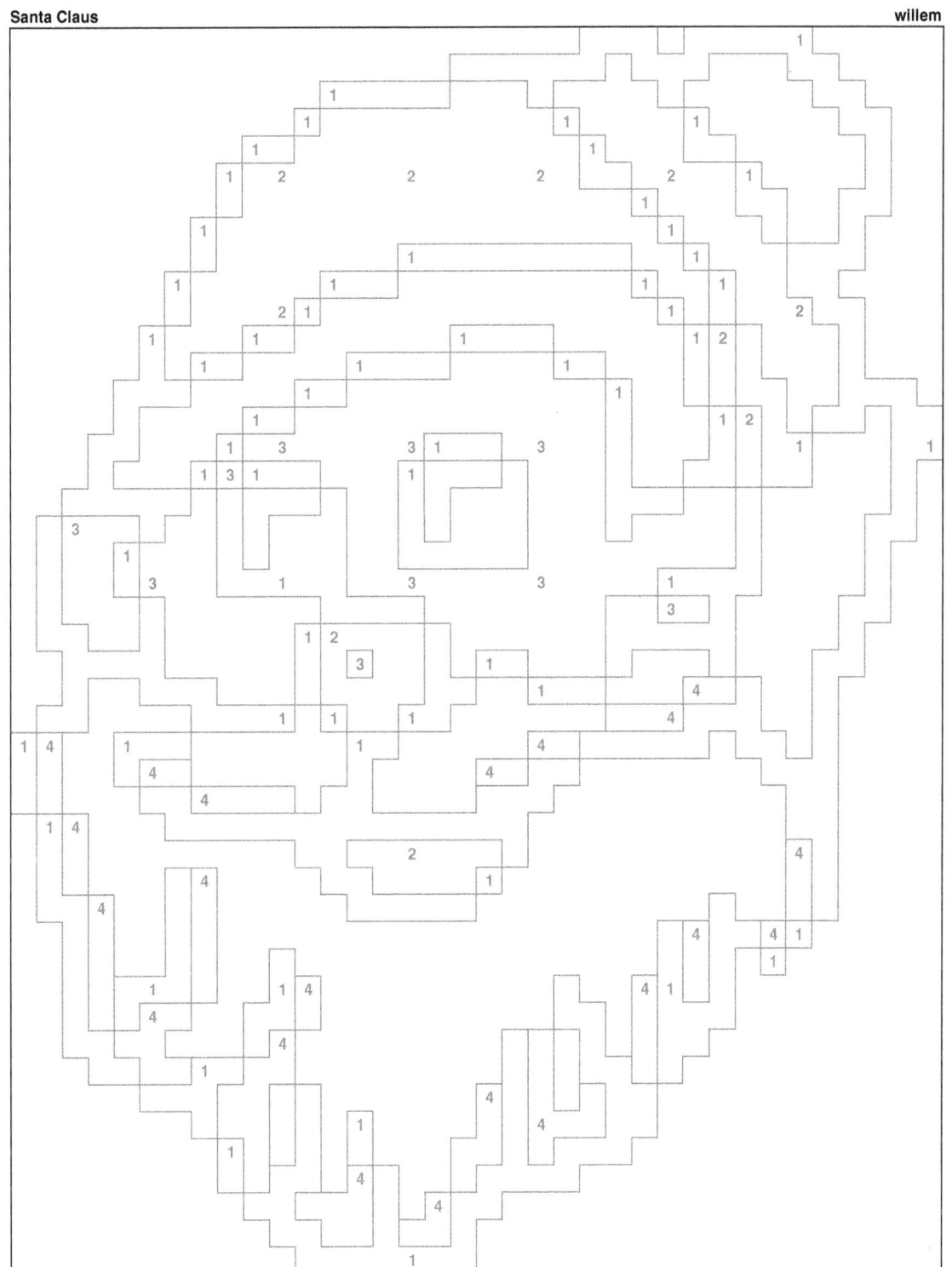

1-Black, 2-Scarlet, 3-Pig Pink, 4-Timberwolf

1-Black, 2-Denim, 3-Manatee, 4-Dandelion, 5-Scarlet

Cat

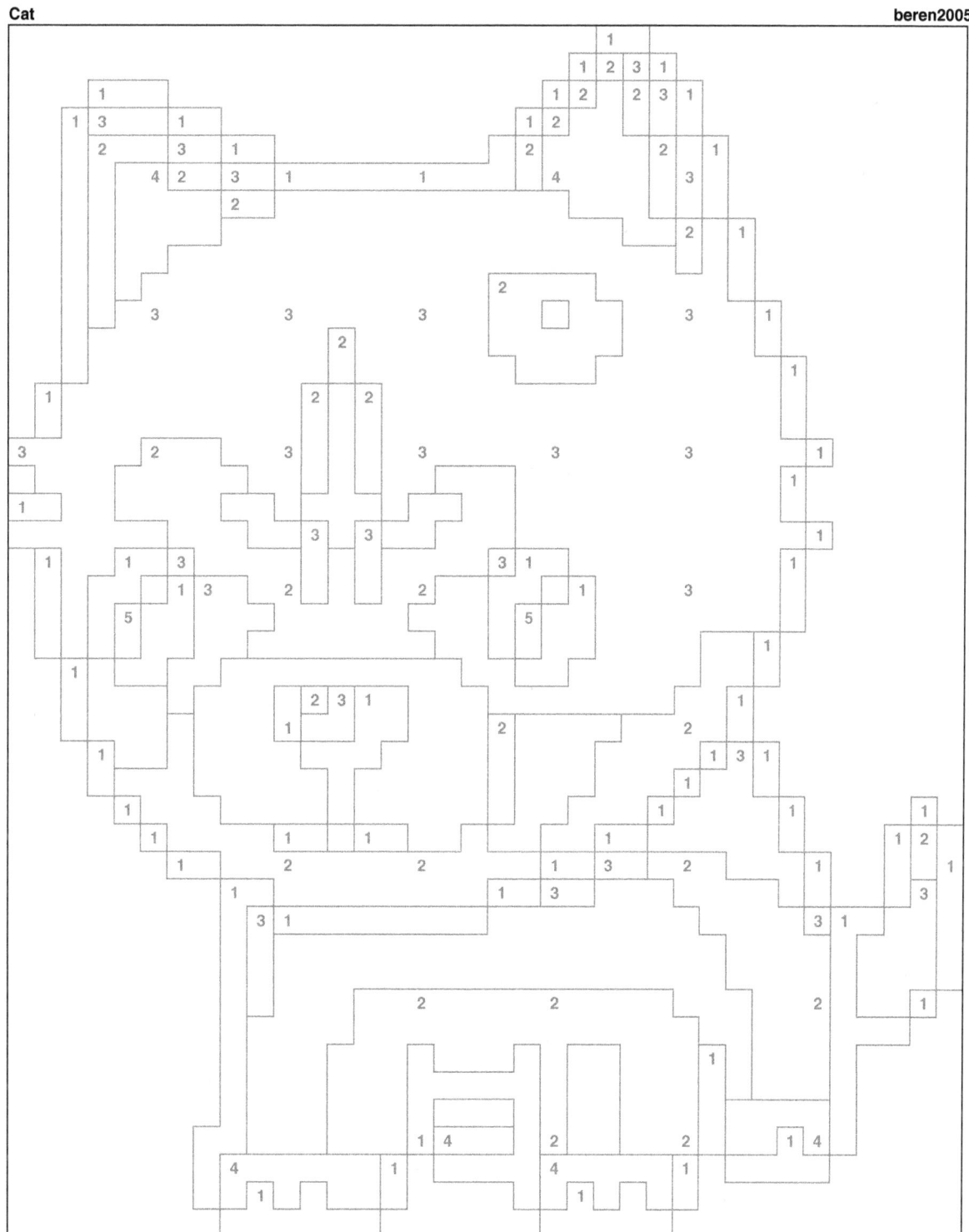

1-Black, 2-Periwinkle, 3-Manatee, 4-Fuzzy Wuzzy, 5-Navy Blue

David McCallum — mudshark

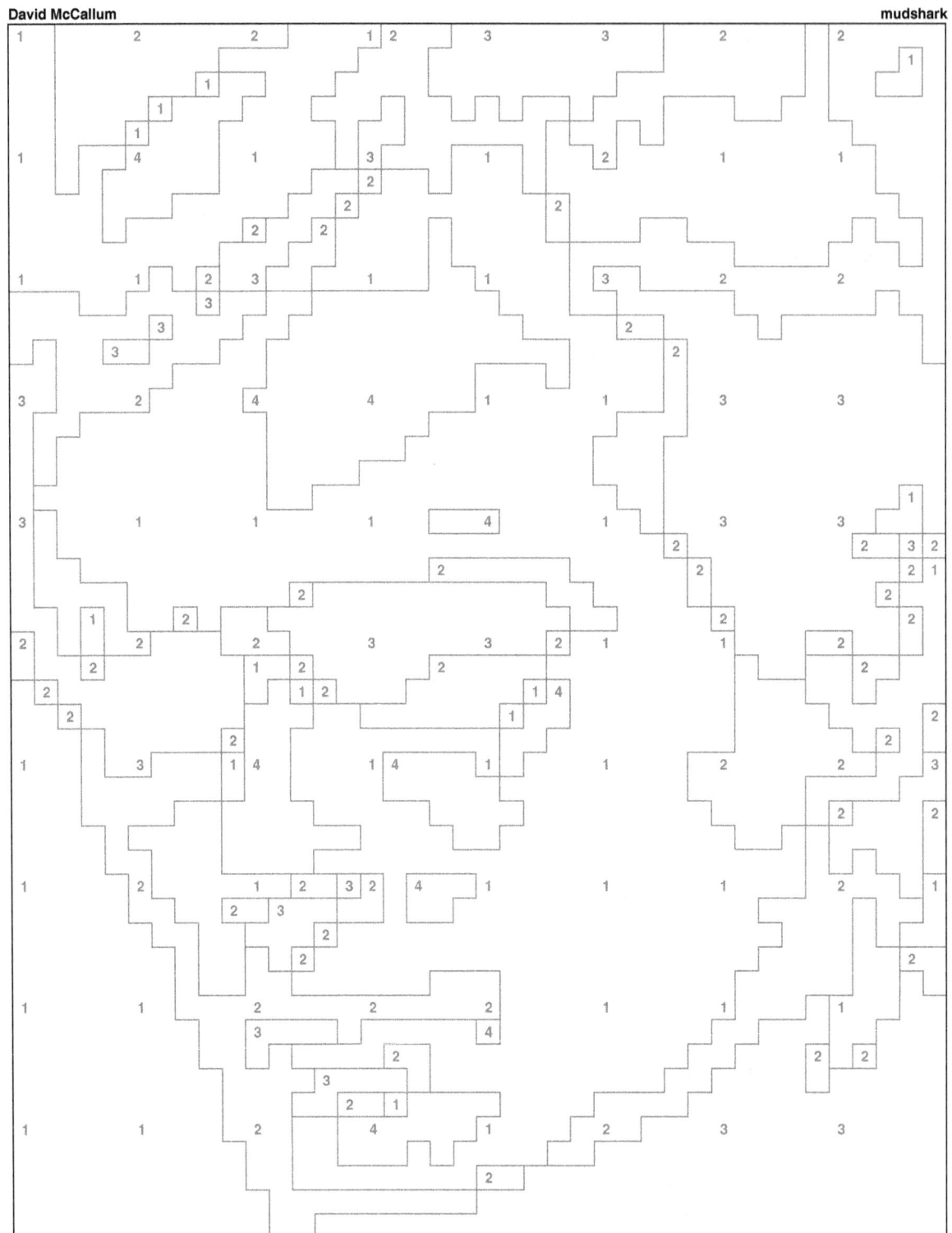

1-Cadet Blue, 2-Eggplant, 3-Black, 4-White

Hedgehog kendrasong

1-Black, 2-Fuzzy Wuzzy, 3-Tumbleweed, 4-Desert Sand, 5-Brown

Wireshark   beren2005

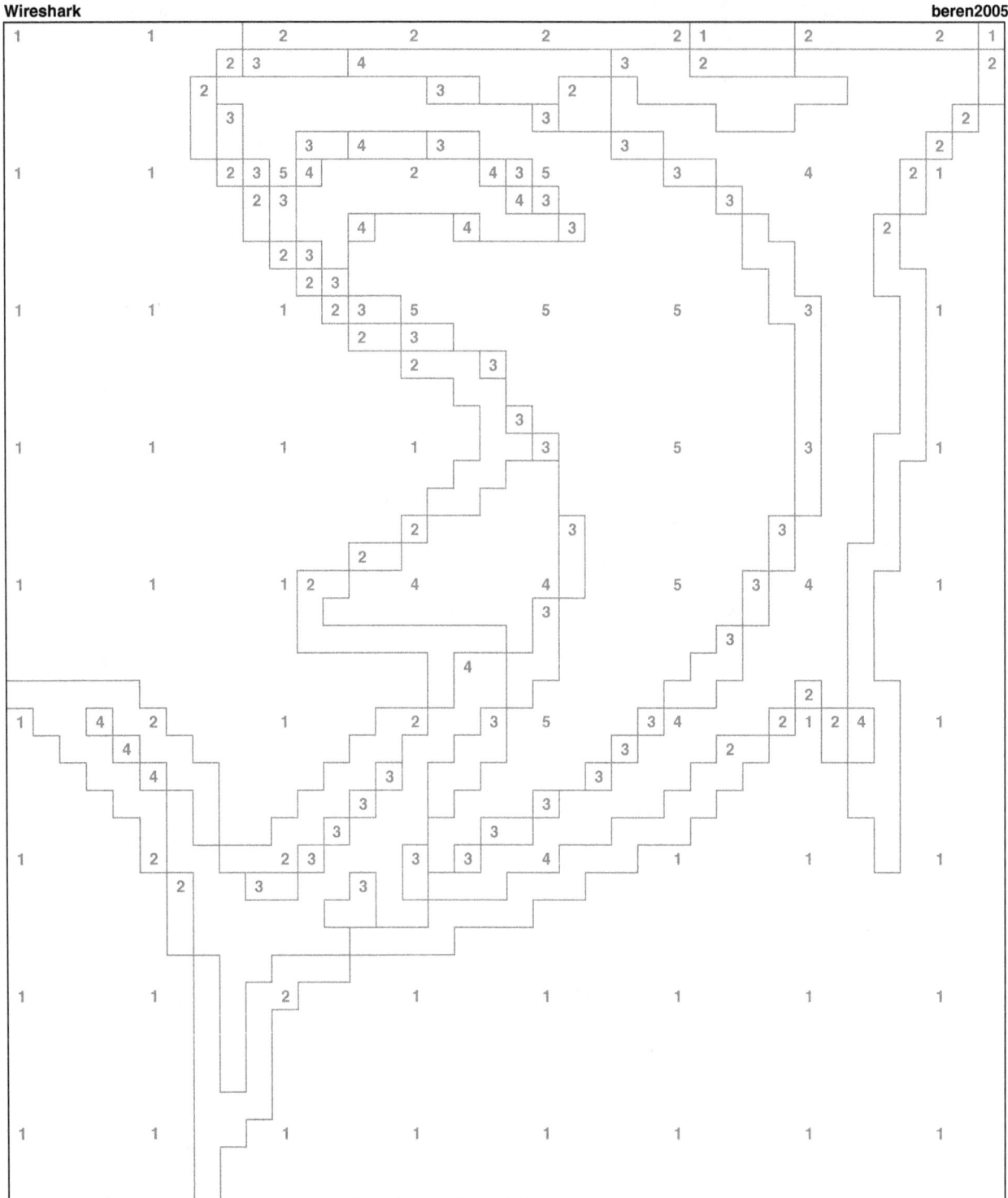

1-Aquamarine, 2-Black, 3-Timberwolf, 4-Cerulean, 5-White

1-Periwinkle, 2-Green, 3-Tropical Rain Forest, 4-Black, 5-White, 6-Mango Tango

He Shouldn't be Here! popkin

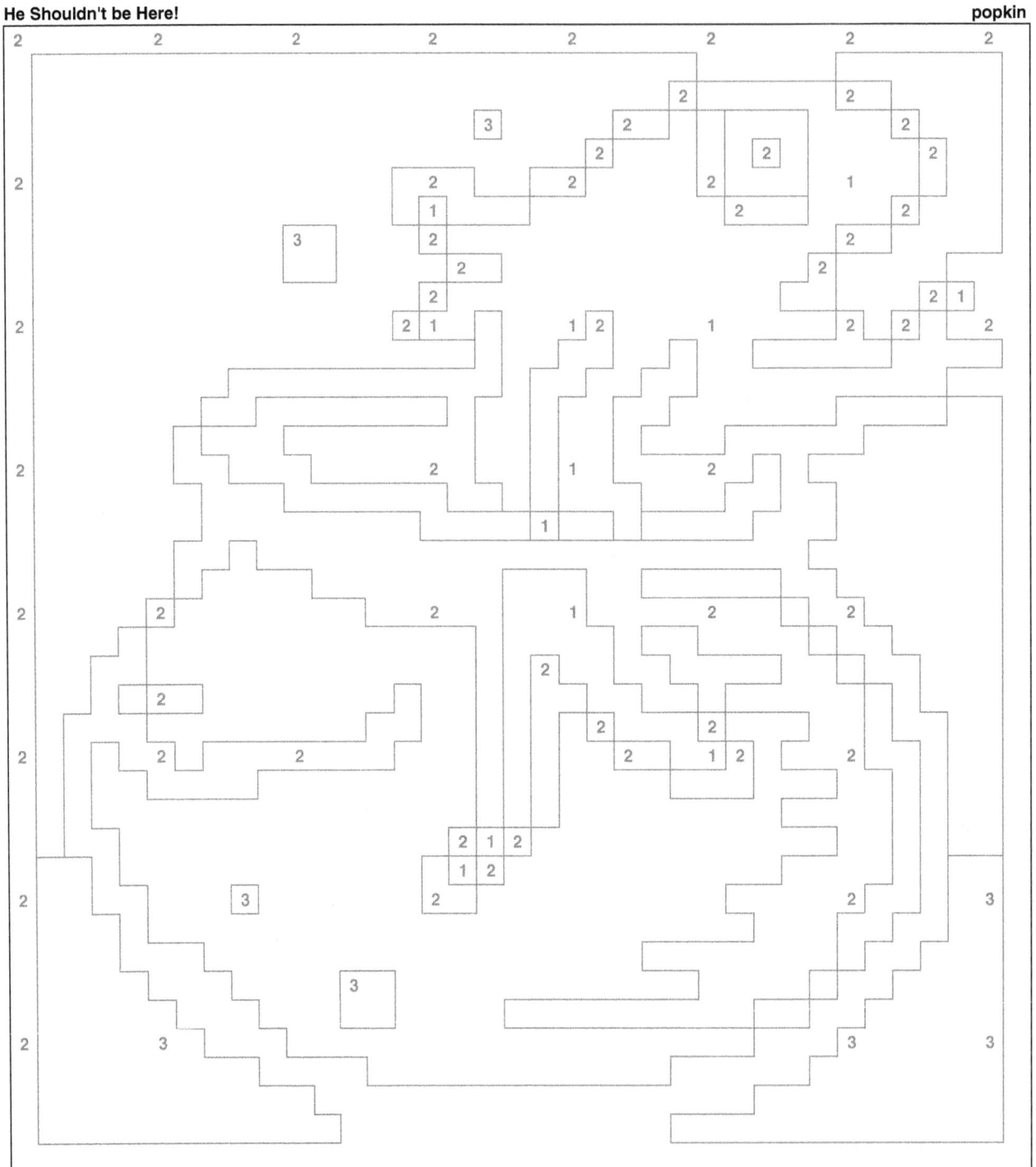

1-Salmon, 2-Black, 3-Robin's Egg Blue

Spring Daisy

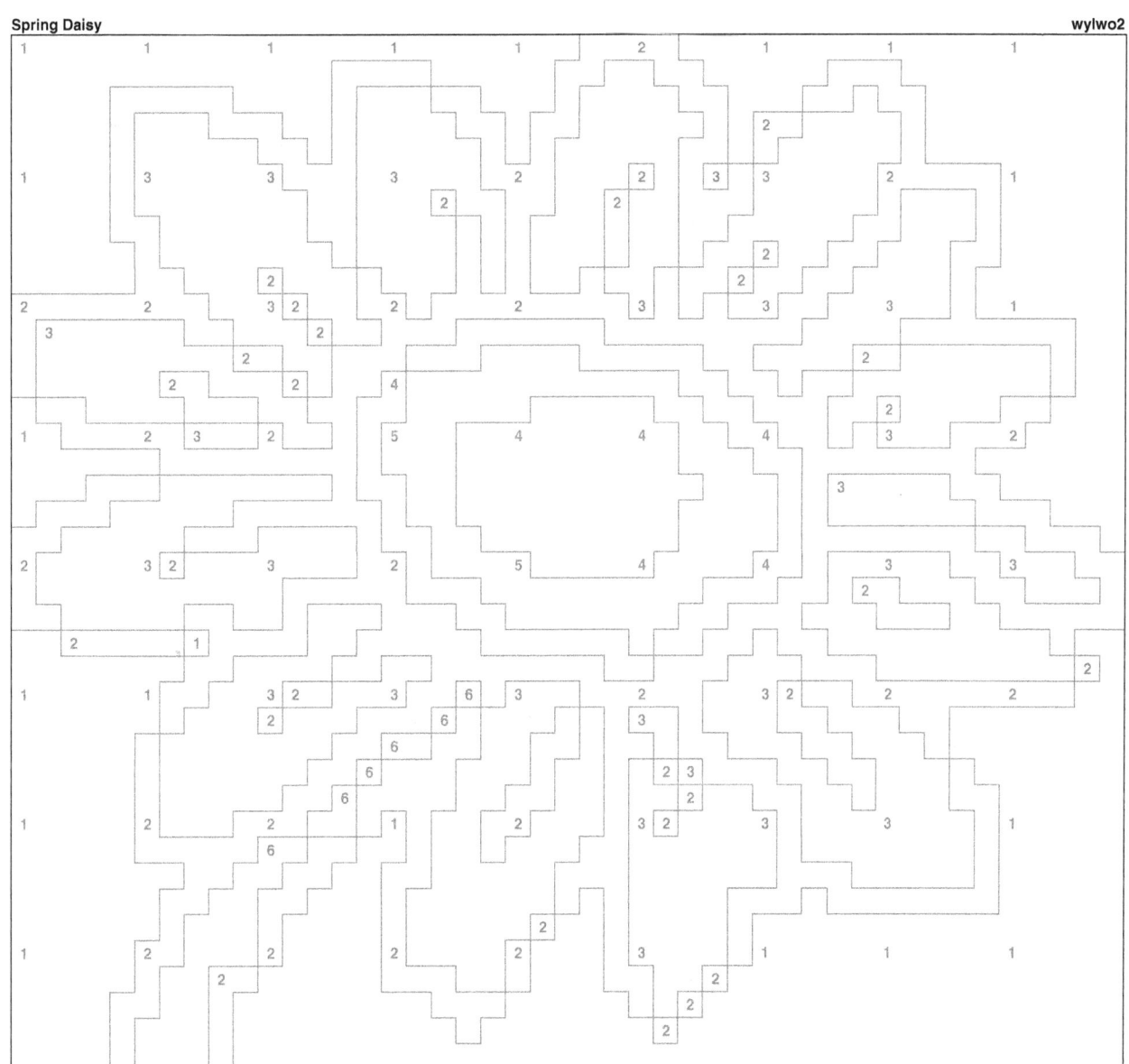

1-Navy Blue, 2-Black, 3-White, 4-Mango Tango, 5-Yellow-Orange, 6-Tropical Rain Forest

Mr. Flibble is Very Cross popkin

1-Black, 2-Blue-Green, 3-Scarlet, 4-Peach, 5-Yellow

www.griddlers.net   **Paint by Numbers, Vol. 1**

Missile, Ghost Trick

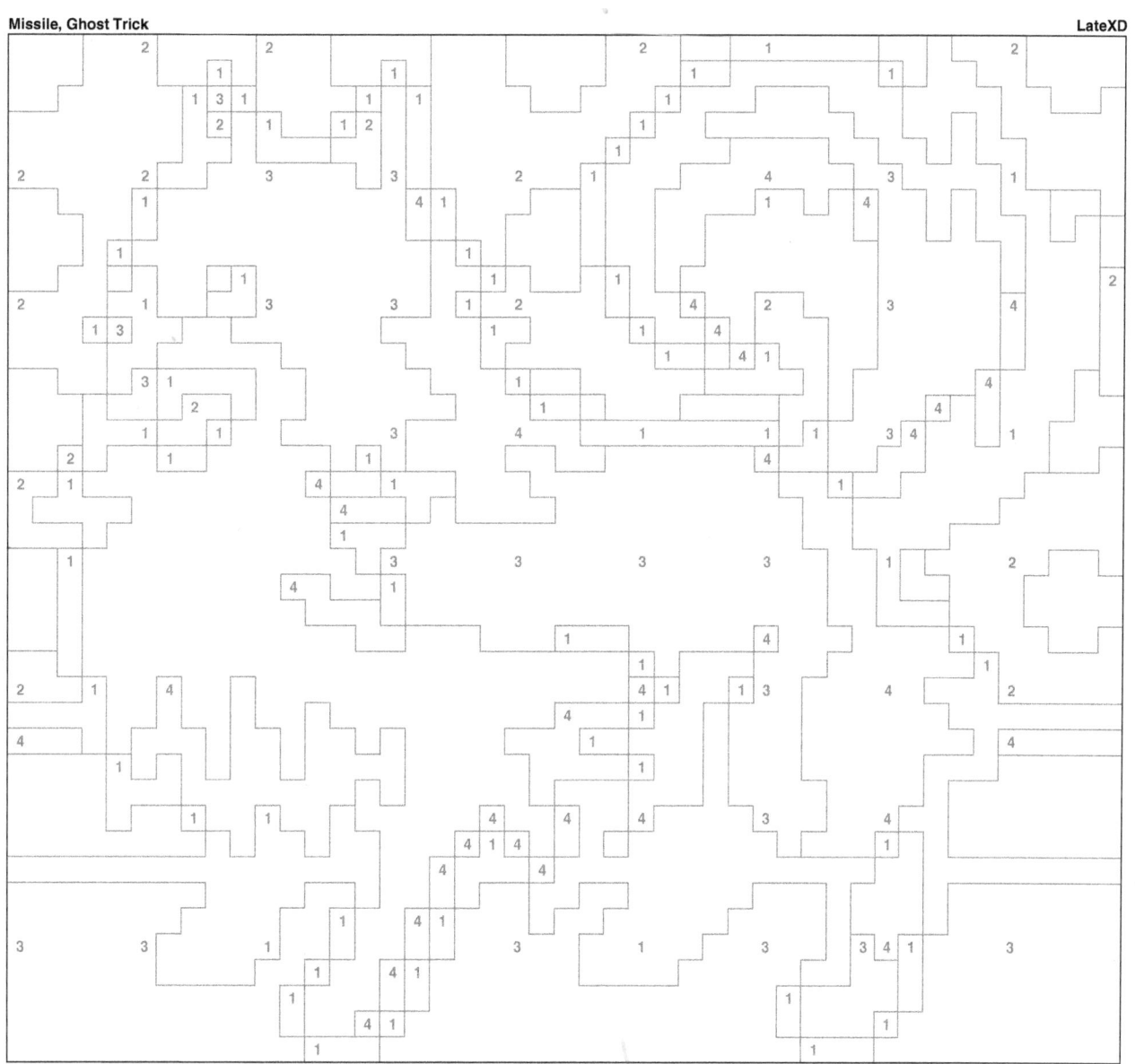

1-Black, 2-Carnation Pink, 3-Burnt Orange, 4-Manatee

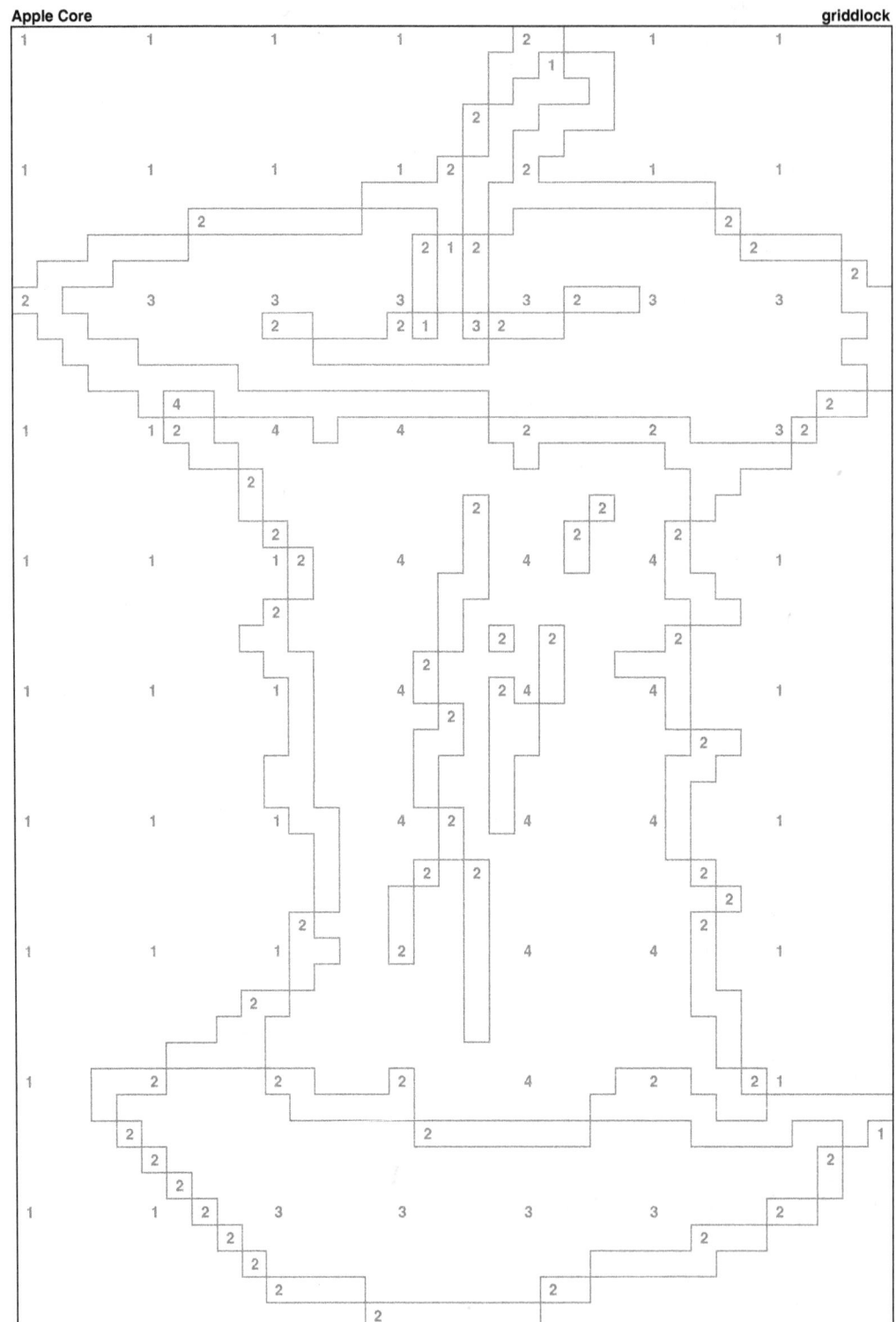

Stork at Dusk Rainbow15

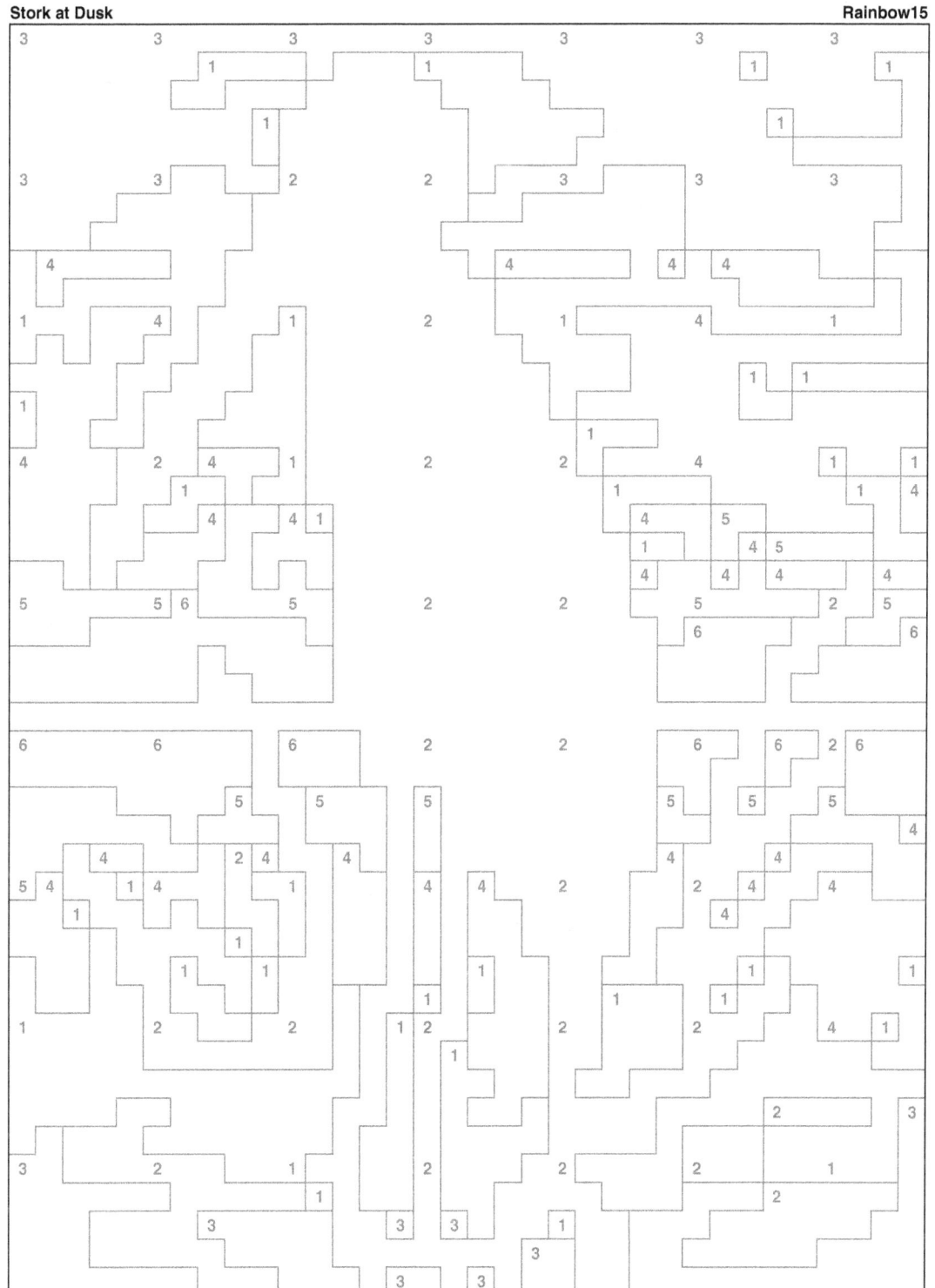

1-Red-Orange, 2-Black, 3-Mango Tango, 4-Maroon, 5-Jazzberry Jam, 6-Purple Heart

Look into Your Heart — Amoebe

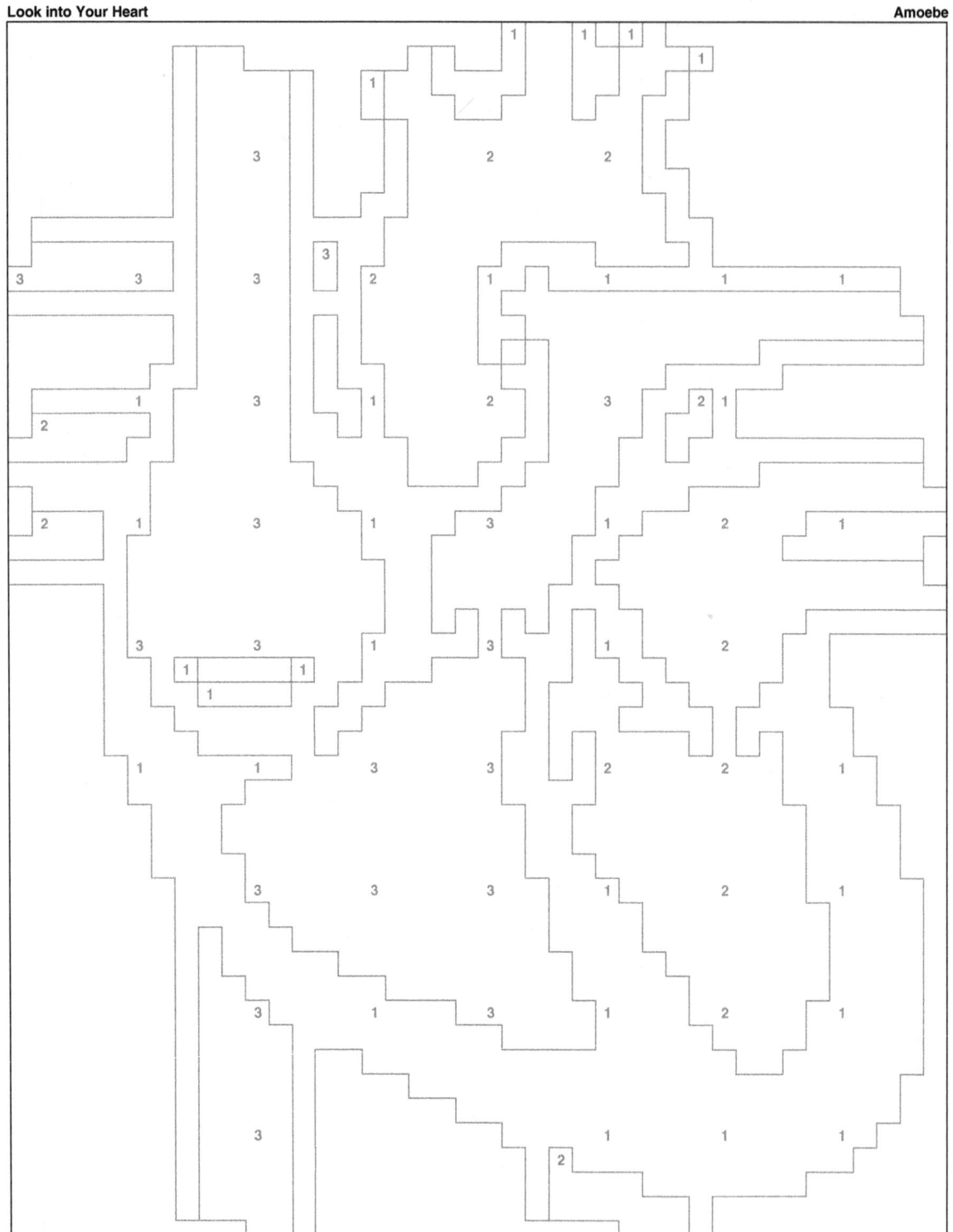

1-Black, 2-Bittersweet, 3-Cornflower

Currant   **Lenchik**

1-Black, 2-Green, 3-Brown, 4-Scarlet

Bambi

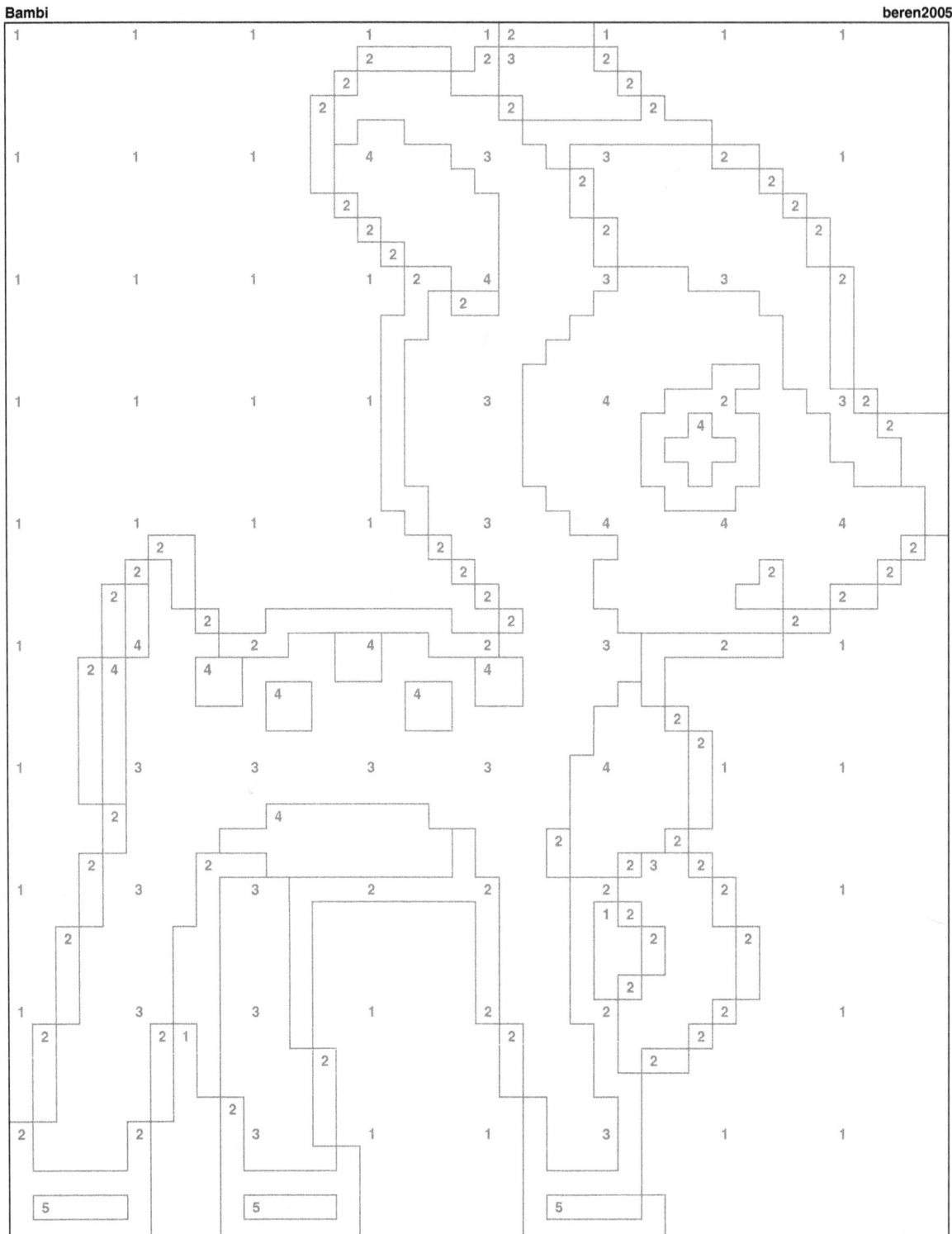

1-Fern, 2-Black, 3-Brown, 4-Banana Mania, 5-Fuzzy Wuzzy

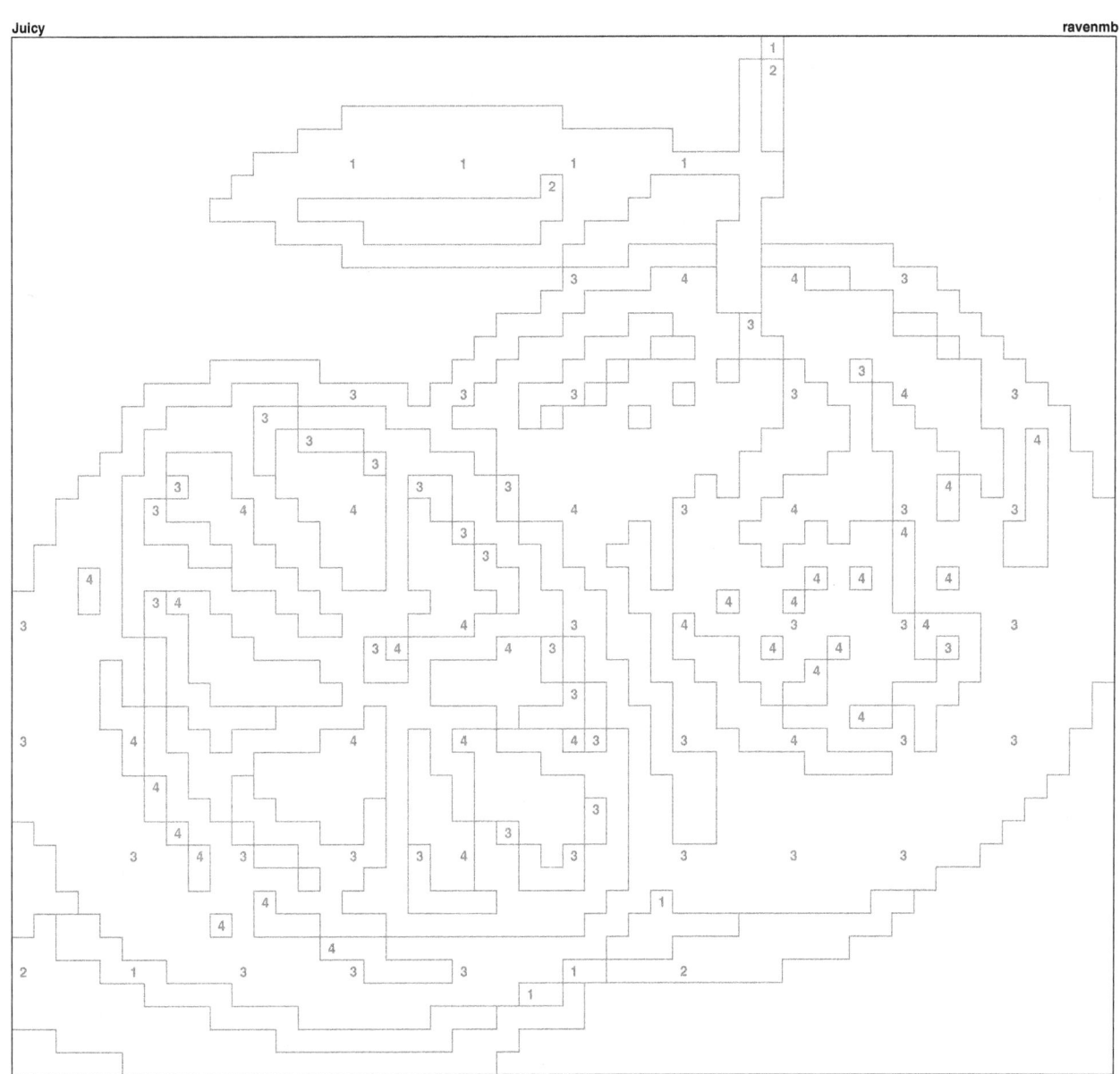

1-Outer Space, 2-Asparagus, 3-Red-Orange, 4-Yellow-Orange

Chimpanzee

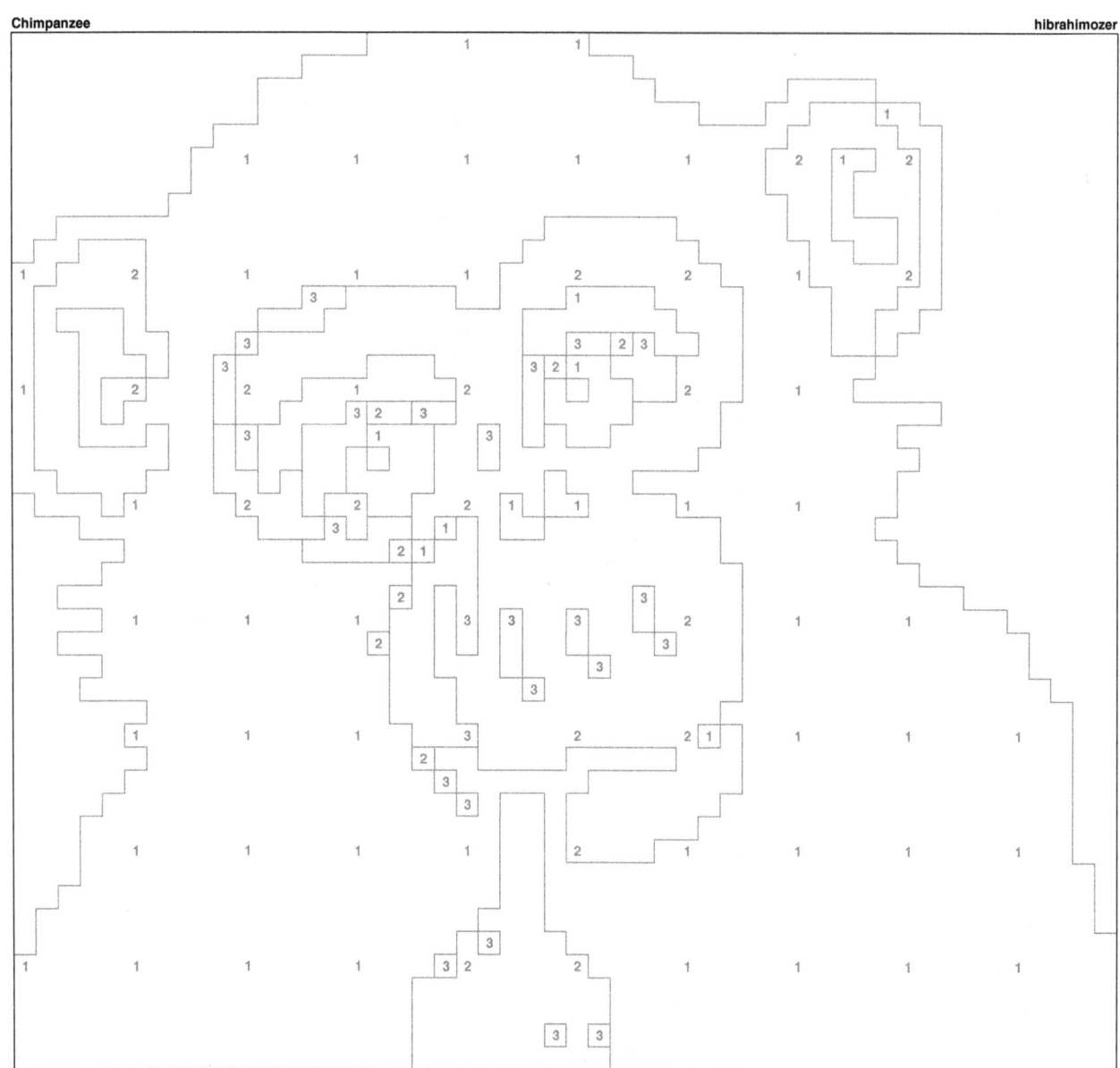

1-Black, 2-Yellow-Orange, 3-Raw Sienna

Sunset Oak — Christophine

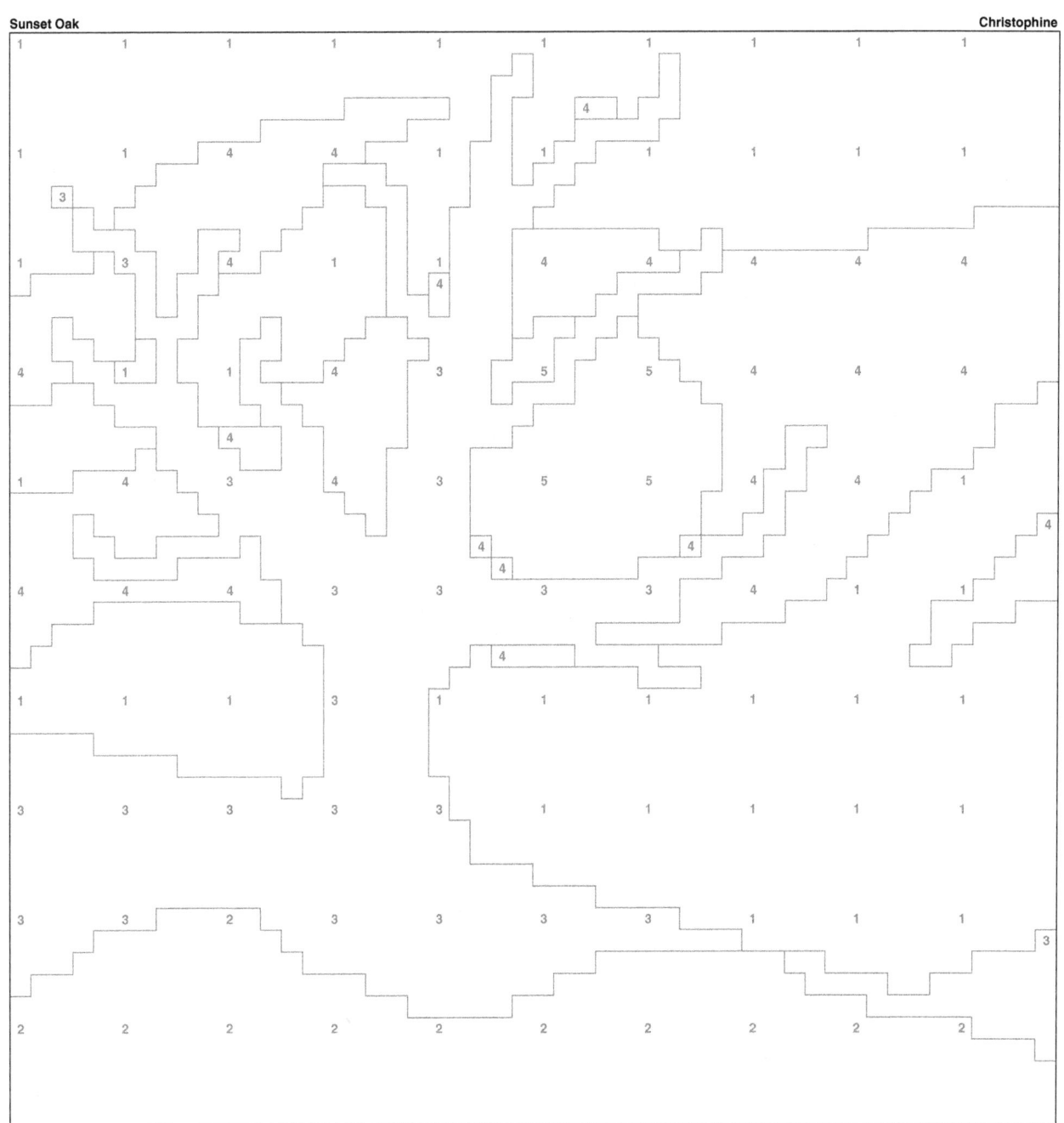

1-Raw Sienna, 2-Eggplant, 3-Black, 4-Yellow-Orange, 5-Dandelion

Paint Tube

1-Black, 2-Manatee, 3-Pacific Blue, 4-Scarlet, 5-Navy Blue

Daisy

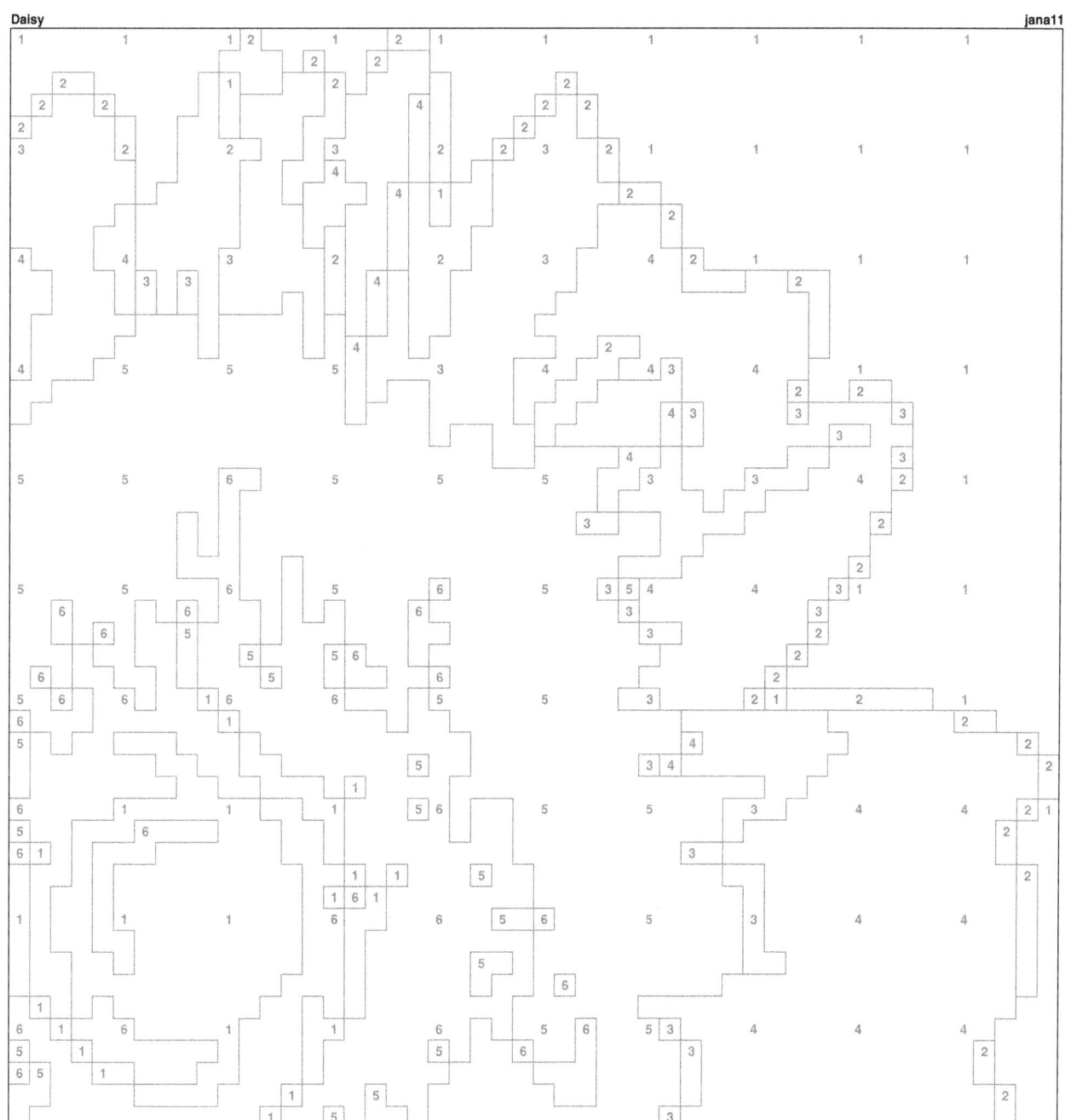

1-Black, 2-Shadow, 3-Olive Green, 4-Green-Yellow, 5-Red, 6-Fuzzy Wuzzy

Pinkie (Gainsborough) popkin

1-Tropical Rain Forest, 2-Fuzzy Wuzzy, 3-White, 4-Salmon, 5-Pig Pink

Storm willem

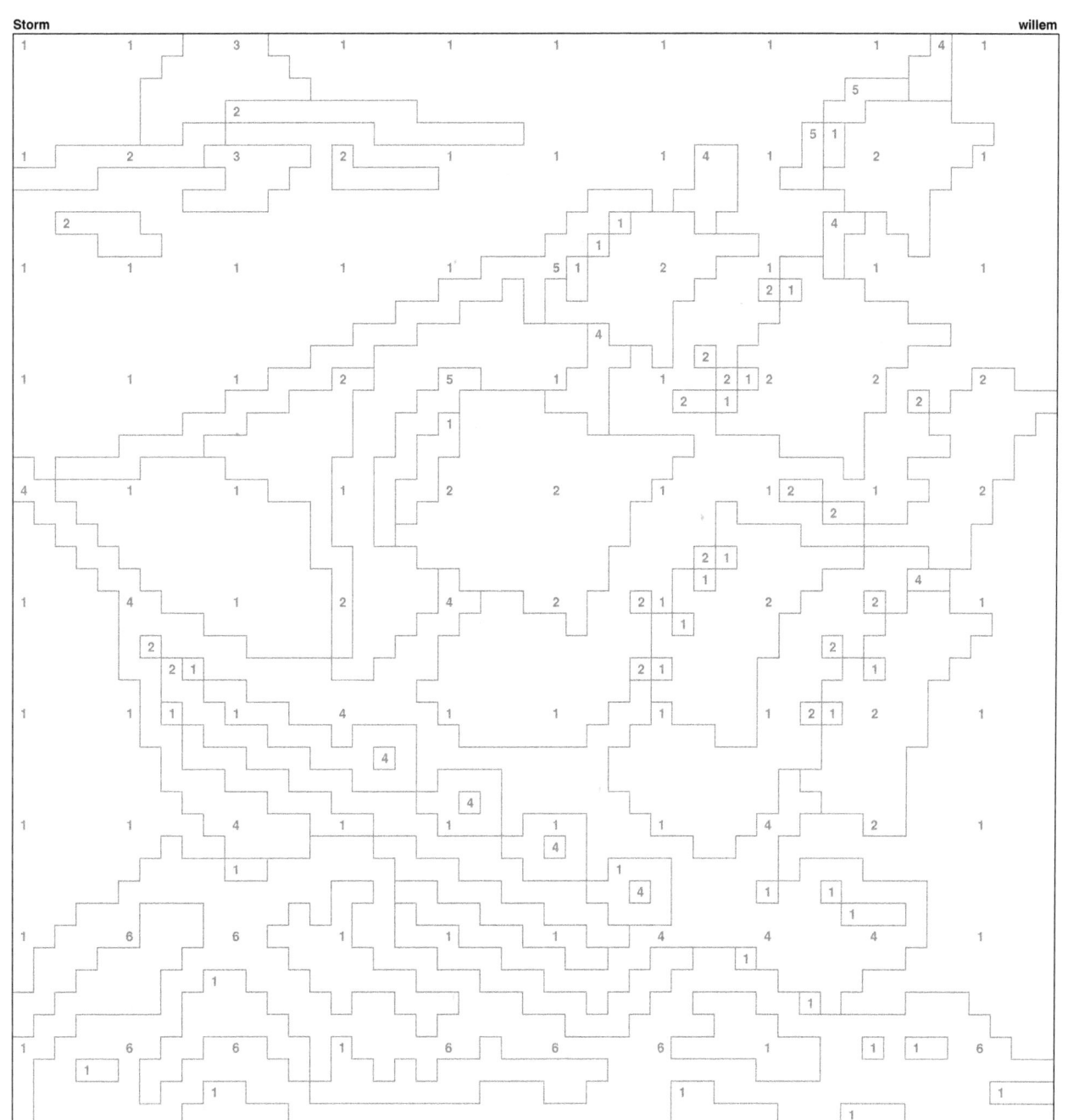

1-Black, 2-Cadet Blue, 3-Inchworm, 4-Fuzzy Wuzzy, 5-Timberwolf, 6-Midnight Blue

Crane Operator stetsonic

1-Black, 2-Yellow-Orange, 3-Dandelion

Steam Engine

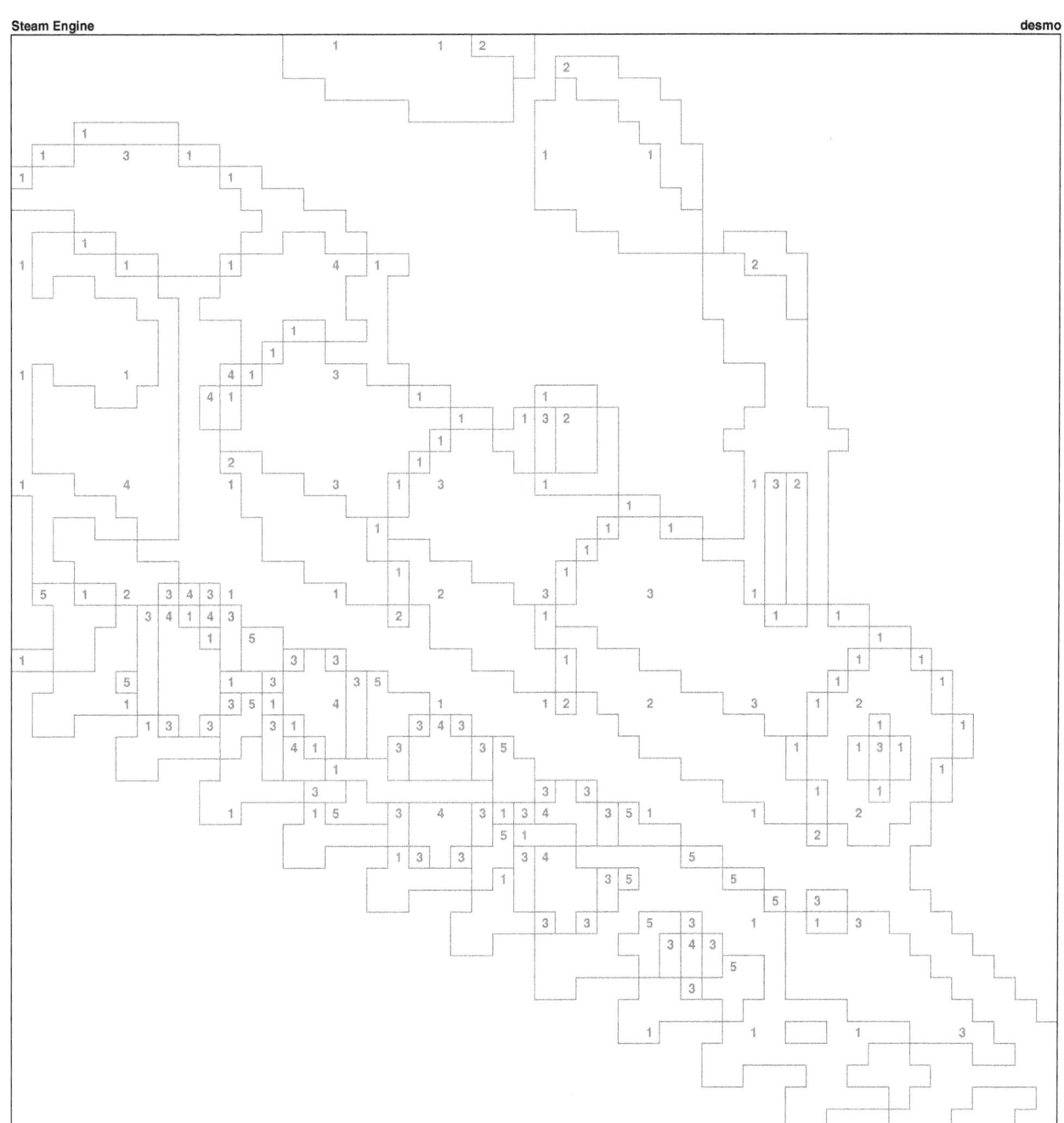

1-Black, 2-Shadow, 3-Timberwolf, 4-Manatee, 5-Eggplant

Stonehenge kikiki

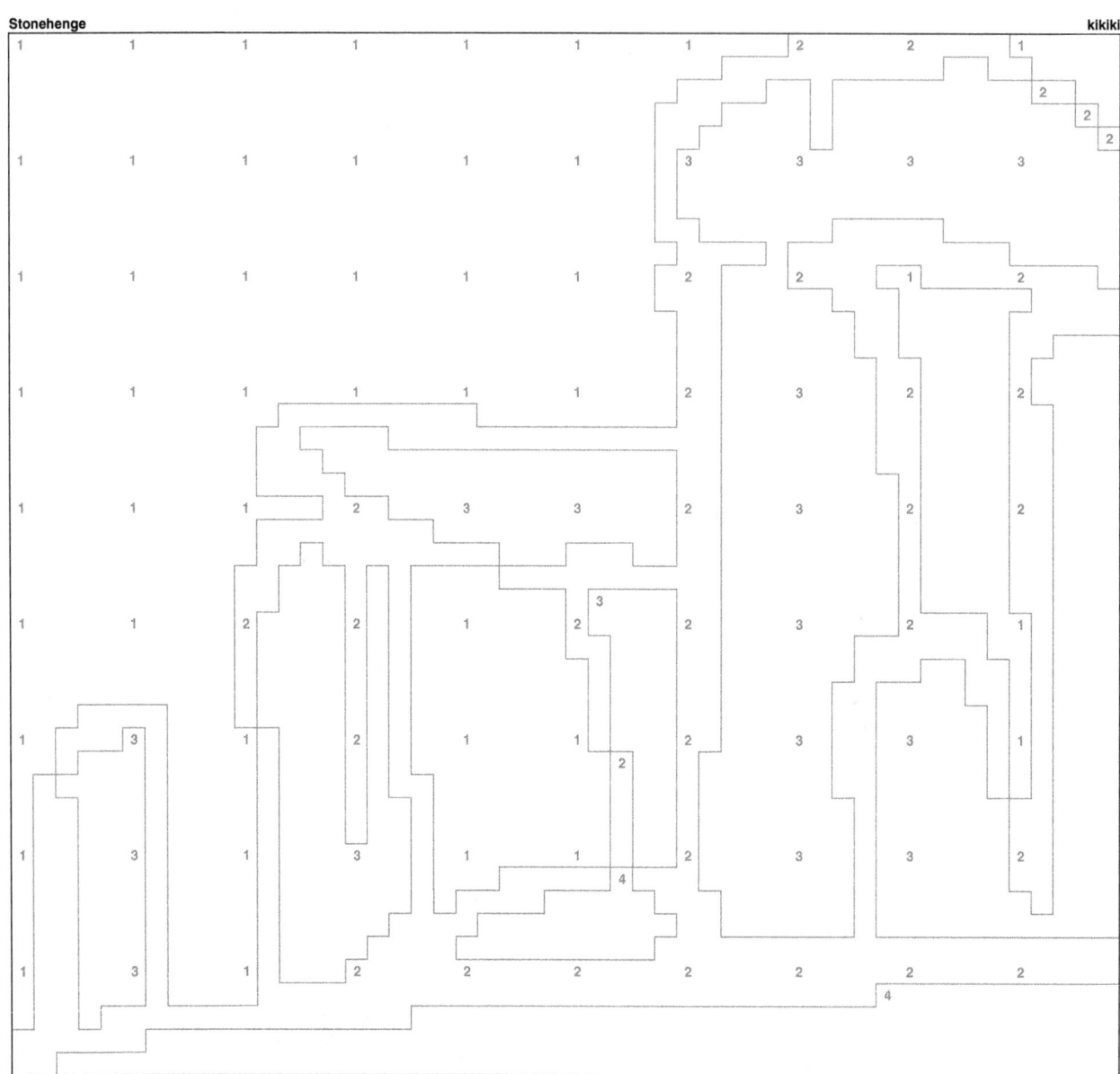

1-Sky Blue, 2-Black, 3-Beaver, 4-Tropical Rain Forest

Stonehenge kikiki

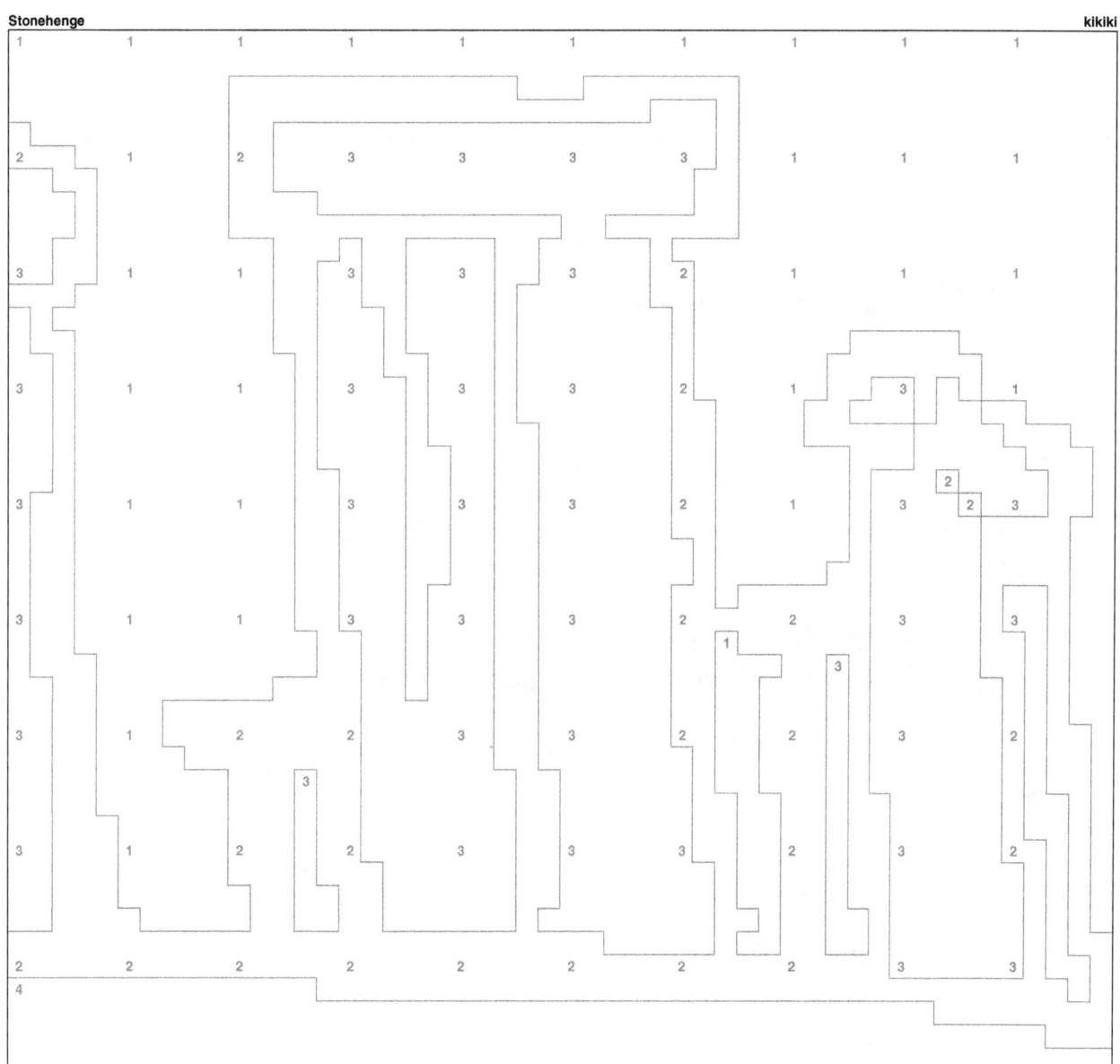

1-Sky Blue, 2-Black, 3-Beaver, 4-Tropical Rain Forest

griddlers
Logic Puzzles

Picture Logic Puzzles:

Griddlers
Griddlers are picture logic puzzles in which cells in a grid have to be colored or left blank according to numbers given at the side of the grid to reveal a hidden picture.

Triddlers
Triddlers are logic puzzles, similar to Griddlers, with the same basic rules of solving. In Triddlers the clues encircle the entire grid. The direction of the clues is horizontal, vertical, or diagonal.

MultiGriddlers
MultiGriddlers are large puzzles that consist of several parts of common griddlers. A Multi can have 2 to 100 parts. The parts are bundled and, once completed, create a bigger picture.

Word Search Puzzles:

Word Search
Word Search is a word game that is letters of a word in a grid. The goal of the game is to find and mark all the words hidden inside the grid. The words may appear horizontally, vertically or diagonally, from top to bottom or bottom to top, from left to right or right to left. A list of the hidden words is provided.

Each puzzle has some text and underscores (_ _ _) to indicate missing word(s). If the puzzle was solved successfully, the remaining letters pop up in the grid and the missing words appear in the text.

Smart Things Begin With Griddlers.net

Number Logic Puzzles:

Sudoku
Sudoku is a logic-based, number-placement puzzle. The goal is to fill a grid with digits so that each column and each row contain the digits only once.

Irregular Blocks (Jigsaws)
Jigsaw puzzle is played the same as Sudoku, except that the grid has Irregular Blocks, also known as cages.

Killer Sudoku
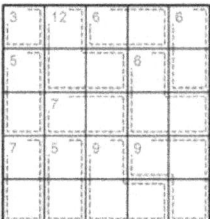
The grid of the **Killer Sudoku** is covered by cages (groups of cells), marked with dotted outlines. Each cage encloses 2 or more cells. The top-left cell is labeled with a cage sum, which is the sum of all solution digits for the cells inside the cage.

Kakuro

Kakuro is played on a grid of filled and barred cells, "black" and "white" respectively. The grid is divided into "entries" (lines of white cells) by the black cells. The black cells contain a slash from upper-left to lower-right and a number in one or both halves. These numbers are called "clues".

Binary
Complete the grid with zeros (0's) and ones (1's) until there are just as many zeros and ones in every row and every column.

Smart Things Begin With Griddlers.net

griddlers Logic Puzzles

Number Logic Puzzles:

Greater Than / Less Than
Greater Than (or **Less Than**) Sudoku has no given clues (digits). Instead, there are "Greater Than" (>) or "Less Than" (<) signs between adjacent cells, which signify that the digit in one cell should be greater than or less than another.

Futoshiki
Futoshiki is played on a grid that may show some digits at the start. Additionally, there are "Greater Than" (>) or "Less Than" (<) signs between adjacent cells, which signify that the digit in one cell should be greater than or less than another.

Kalkudoku
The grid of the **Kalkudoku** is divided into heavily outlined cages (groups of cells). The numbers in the cells of each cage must produce a certain "target" number when combined using a specified mathematical operation (either addition, subtraction, multiplication or division).

Straights
Straights (**Str8ts**) is played on a grid that is partially divided by black cells into compartments. Compartments must contain a straight - a set of consecutive numbers - but in any order (for example: 2-1-3-4). There can also be white clues in black cells.

Skyscrapers

The **Skyscrapers** puzzle has numbers along the edge of the grid. Those numbers indicate the number of buildings which you would see from that direction if there was a series of skyscrapers with heights equal the entries in that row or column.

Smart Things Begin With Griddlers.net